Also available from Continuum

The Teaching Assistant's Guide to Managing Behaviour

Jill Morgan

continuum

Continuum International Publishing Group
The Tower Building   80 Maiden Lane
11 York Road   Suite 704
London SE1 7NX   New York, NY 10038

www.continuumbooks.com

British Library Cataloguing-in-Publication Data
A catalogue record for this book is available from the British Library.

ISBN: 9-780-8264-9682-9 (paperback)

Typeset by Kenneth Burnley, Wirral, Cheshire
Printed and bound in England by Antony Rowe Ltd, Chippenham, Wilts

Contents

Appendix 135

Contents

List of Figures

List of Tables

Introduction

This book has been written for Teaching Assistants, many thousands of whom work in schools throughout the world, supporting the teaching and learning process. If you are one of those TAs, I hope you recognize the essential nature of the work you perform. You may be known as a Teaching Assistant, a Classroom Assistant or an LSA – or by one of several other titles. You may work in a mainstream setting, or a special school. You may be new to the job or an old hand at it. You may have received fairly extensive training for your job, or relatively little. Whichever of these is true, as a TA you make a significant difference to the lives of children. This book – and the others which make up the series – has been written to help you in your work as you support your supervising teacher and the pupils who are assigned to you.

Why behaviour management for TAs?

You are employed as a TA – a *teaching* assistant – so is behaviour management part of your role, and an appropriate responsibility? The only answer to that is an unequivocal 'Yes'. Behaviour management may or may not be listed on your job description, but it is one of your responsibilities. Every adult who works with children automatically has responsibility for managing behaviour. In fact, we all use behaviour management in our daily interactions with other people, whether we realize it or not. We adapt the way we speak, make requests, or respond to other people's demands according to who we are with, and what we are hoping to achieve from the encounter. As we interact with other people we constantly affect each other's behaviour. This book is intended to help you in your interactions with pupils, so that you can achieve the best outcomes for them – so that you can manage their behaviour and your own in a way which will maximize learning and minimize distractions.

There is an important point to add here. As a TA you work under the direction of a teacher or other professional designated as your supervisor. Read this book with that principle constantly in mind. Although the basic principles of behaviour management are explained in this book, you are not expected to devise behaviour management systems – you must work within your supervising teacher's existing system and preferences. The principles have been explained so that you can better understand why your teacher works in a particular way, and so that you can use them as you work with groups and individual pupils. But always make a point of following your teacher's lead, and asking for clarification if you do not understand your role. Use the principles, but do not exceed your responsibilities.

As a TA you work under the direction of a teacher or other professional designated as your supervisor.

What do we mean by behaviour?

Behaviour is what people do, and behaviours are like verbs – doing words. We could substitute the word *actions* for *behaviour*. Think of stick-figure drawings – playing football, reading a book, dancing, skipping or swimming. If you work with teenagers, some of these behaviours may sound too active for your pupils, who are more likely to be hanging out with their friends or listening to music. But even these fairly passive activities would qualify as verbs, and would be considered behaviours – as would thinking, watching and listening. If you had to write a list of all the behaviours you see in the classroom on a daily basis, it would be very long. A small selection is listed in the box.

Behaviours include:

running	jumping	talking
reading	laughing	raising a hand to speak
hitting	swearing	singing
writing	painting	asking a question

Notice that some of the behaviours in the box would be considered positive and appropriate for the classroom, others less so. But this is a book about managing behaviour, and that means all behaviour – appropriate and inappropriate, good and bad.

There is a tendency when we talk about behaviour management to immediately think of inappropriate or challenging behaviour. We picture the difficult pupils whose behaviour tests our patience and ingenuity – those who threaten the smooth working of the classroom and disrupt our teaching, and the other pupils' learning. But the primary purpose of behaviour management is to establish and maintain appropriate behaviour. When we think of the well-behaved pupils in our classes and groups, we really do not associate the term 'behaviour management' with them because their behaviour does not seem to need managing – they seem to manage it well enough themselves. But all classrooms – even those which seem to be full of motivated, polite and compliant pupils – need a definite and deliberate behaviour management plan. As we will discuss later in the book, there must be consequences identified for all behaviour – good and bad – and the well-behaved pupils will maintain better behaviour if they can see that there is a system of rewards or positive consequences in place for them, as well as negative consequences for pupils who misbehave. Behaviour management is both a carrot and a stick, but it is first and most importantly the carrot: how your interactions with pupils encourage and support appropriate behaviour.

> The primary purpose of behaviour management is to establish and maintain appropriate behaviour.

What we now call behaviour or classroom management was formerly referred to as *discipline* – a word strongly associated with punishment, although the word has nothing negative in its origins. It stems from the Latin word for a pupil, and its closest word in modern English is *disciple* – a follower or learner. The word 'discipline' in its wider meaning includes training, or controlling and regulating behaviour – which is the sense in which it will be used in this book.

In 1989 the government published the Elton Report. Officially entitled the *Report of the Committee of Enquiry into Discipline in Schools*, it marked an important point in education in the UK, because it stressed the very real link between behaviour and learning. The more recent 2005 government report on behaviour in schools – the Steer Report – is entitled *Learning Behaviour* (see the appendix for details). This title extends the behaviour-learning link identified in the Elton Report, and has two facets:

1. It suggests that you are working in an environment where children are learning how to behave (and by implication, where you as one of the adults are teaching them how to behave).
2. It reaffirms the direct connection between behaviour and learning, emphasizing the need to actively encourage the type of behaviour that is conducive to learning.

The Steer Report is also based on six core beliefs, which are listed in the box. These are very substantial statements about behaviour and behaviour management in schools, and we will revisit them in the different chapters of the book.

In March 2005 Ofsted, the government body responsible for school standards and inspections, produced a report called *Managing Challenging Behaviour*. Among other things, it stated:

> The great majority of children and young people enjoy learning, work hard and behave well.

Steer Report – Core Beliefs

1. The quality of learning, teaching and behaviour are inseparable issues, and are the responsibility of all staff.
2. Poor behaviour cannot be tolerated – it is a denial of the rights of pupils to learn and teachers to teach. To enable learning to take place, preventative action is most effective, but where this fails, schools must have clear, firm and intelligent strategies in place to help pupils manage their behaviour.
3. There is no single solution to the problem of poor behaviour, but all schools have the potential to raise standards if they are consistent in implementing good practice in learning, teaching and behaviour management.
4. Respect has to be given in order to be received. Parents and carers, pupils and teachers all need to operate in a culture of mutual regard.
5. The support of parents is essential for the maintenance of good behaviour. Parents and schools each need to have a clear understanding of their rights and responsibilities.
6. School leaders have a critical role in establishing high standards of learning, teaching and behaviour.

Among the schools inspected by Ofsted in the 2003/4 school year, behaviour was considered 'good' or better in 90 per cent of primary schools, 68 per cent of secondary schools and 80 per cent of special schools and Pupil Referral Units (PRUs). This is very encouraging, and hopefully matches your own experience. The report also stated that:

- Most pupils' behaviour is satisfactory or good; most schools manage behaviour well.
- The most common – and most wearing – form of bad behaviour is the persistent 'low-level' type of disruption that interferes with teaching and learning; extreme violence is very rare and committed by very few pupils.
- Some pupils – and they are usually boys – do behave in ways that cause serious concern because they have a detrimental effect on learning – for those pupils and for others around them.
- Many pupils who exhibit problem behaviour also have special needs and may come from unsupportive and difficult family backgrounds.

Take a mental look around the classrooms where you work. How would you describe the behaviour that you see? Is it, as Ofsted reported, generally well managed and acceptable? And is the unacceptable behaviour mostly of the mildly irritating sort, and generated by a minority of pupils who disrupt teaching and learning? What about the pupils with special needs and those who come from dysfunctional families – do they present particular challenges for you and your teacher? You will find information on each of these points in the chapters that follow, with specific strategies that you can use in your supportive role as a TA.

Your role in behaviour management

So what exactly is your role? In its most general sense, it is to assist in managing behaviour. As for the specific details, that is something that this book cannot tell you because your precise role and responsibilities are determined by the school or setting in which you work, within a framework set by your local authority (LA). And the minute daily details of what you should do in relation to behaviour management are determined by the teacher or other designated supervisor under whose direction you work. If you work in more than one classroom or setting, this may mean that expectations differ according to which classroom you are in. So how do you find out what is expected? Basically you have two options:

- trial and error
- ask

The better option is obviously to ask for instruction or direction up front. In reality you will probably use both of these methods to some extent to learn about your role. Even if your teacher gives you a list of your responsibilities, there will always be occasions when you are not sure how to apply his or her directions – when you will have to act on your own judgement and check afterwards whether you have done the right thing. But do ask, and do check if you are not sure. Responsibility comes on more than one level. You may have decision-making responsibilities; you certainly have responsibility for carrying out decisions made by your supervisor. Both are important. So as you read through the information in this book, ask yourself on a regular basis: Is this something that I have responsibility for? At which level do I have that responsibility – making the decisions myself, or supporting my supervisor's decisions?

Structure and outline of the book

This book is designed to guide you through the process of learning basic principles of behaviour management, and applying them to your own work setting. Each chapter is interspersed with opportunities to stop and think about what you have read, to consider your own philosophy and attitudes, and to look for examples of the principles discussed in your own pupils and classrooms. At the end of each chapter there is a self-evaluation section, which guides you through the process of applying one or two of the principles from the chapter in a more detailed way. You may not wish to write on the book, or you may need more space in which to write. If this is the case you can photocopy forms and other relevant pages from the book. Under the terms of copyright it is permissible for you to do this provided the copies are made *for your own use only.* You are encouraged to write down your thoughts and ideas, because the process of writing obliges you to think more carefully about the principles and strategies that you have read about, and how they apply to your pupils. Thus the book becomes a study-guide rather than just reading material.

The content of the book is organized into five chapters. In brief, this is what you can anticipate:

■ First we take a look at behaviour in general, considering some different theoretical perspectives on behaviour. This is where you have a first opportunity to consider your personal philosophy, as well as the factors which influence how children behave, including culture, ability and children's emotional and physical needs.
■ In Chapter 2 we look at the ABCs of behaviour – Antecedents, Behaviour and Consequences: what triggers behaviour, and what are some of the possible results. The important concept in this chapter is that none of this is

fixed; you can influence both the antecedents and the consequences as a TA, and that means you can have a powerful impact on behaviour.

- In Chapter 3 we look at how good teachers set expectations for behaviour by establishing routines and rules, with clearly identified consequences for those who keep rules and those who do not. But we also consider the contribution which good teaching and strong relationships make to a positive learning environment. These are areas which come well within your remit and capabilities.
- Chapter 4 is all about rewards and sanctions. As a TA this is definitely part of your responsibility, because neither good nor bad behaviour should go unnoticed, and if you are the adult working with pupils, then it falls to you to be the one to provide rewards or sanctions.
- In Chapter 5 we look at the different ways that you can encourage and actively teach children to take responsibility for their own behaviour. This is the principle of self-determination – helping children develop a greater sense of awareness about how they act and growing control over it.

The Ofsted Report *Managing Challenging Behaviour* made several recommendations for actions that schools can take to improve behaviour:

- focus on providing appropriate curriculum and improving the quality of teaching
- improve literacy and communication skills
- keep track of pupils' progress in academic and social skills, and use this information to help pupils improve their behaviour
- promote consistency in managing behaviour across the school
- engage the support of parents

■ provide more behaviour management training for staff – including TAs.

Many of these recommendations are outside of your influence as a TA – you do not set the curriculum and you may have no responsibility for working with parents. However, you can take up the challenge to

■ use quality teaching methods
■ provide consistency by following your supervisor's lead
■ help pupils become more aware of and take more responsibility for their own behaviour.

These topics will all be covered in the various chapters of this book. And of course by reading the book you have already begun to take personal responsibility for the last recommendation by seeking to increase your own behaviour management skills.

1

Understanding behaviour

In this chapter we take a look at some different perspectives on behaviour. You will also have an opportunity to consider your own beliefs about children's behaviour and the role of teachers and TAs in shaping that behaviour. This is important because your philosophy (even if you have never referred to your beliefs in this way) largely determines how you react to the different ways your pupils behave, and the extent to which you will be comfortable with your teacher's approach to behaviour management. So we first look at some theories or approaches to behaviour:

- a psychodynamic approach
- behavioural approaches
- a cognitive behavioural approach.

Then we look at some of the factors that influence how pupils act, and what you consider to be acceptable behaviour in school. And lastly we look at the difference culture and special needs might make to the behavioural expectations we may have of our pupils.

Some different theoretical perspectives

The various approaches that have been used to manage behaviour over the years have been based on differing philosophies or views of:

- what behaviour is
- how it is generated or what motivates it
- how we should treat other people (including children) – that is, what their rights and our responsibilities are.

Think back to when you were a child. Were you brought up with the idea that 'children should be seen and not heard'? If you were, then you were probably taught not to interrupt adults or express your opinion without being asked for them, and to address adults quite formally, for example as 'Mr/Mrs', or 'auntie'/'uncle' for your parents' friends. If this is your era, then you would also have been taught to address teachers formally, as a mark of respect. School would have been a place of relative silence – except for playtime – and very structured learning, with a certain amount of chanting or repetition of tables and spellings. If you are of more recent vintage, you may have been brought up with less formal ideas and been encouraged to learn through active discovery, with more freedom to express yourself. Your classroom would probably have buzzed with pupils exchanging ideas (hopefully with a focus on the learning activity) and you may have been encouraged to call your teacher by his or her first name. These differing levels of formality in the classroom would be accompanied by differing expectations of children's behaviour. Behaviours that were considered unacceptable in the more formal approach might be perfectly acceptable in more recent years and less formal classrooms.

If we go back into the nineteenth century or earlier, unacceptable or antisocial behaviour – essentially, behaviour which broke the rules or did not conform to social norms – was usually connected with evil. But children's behaviour did not have to be extreme in order to be punished quite severely. Think of the story of Jane Eyre. Although she is a fictional character, her situation is based on real events from the mid-1800s. Her aunt accused her of being wicked and sent her away to school because of her bad behaviour – which essentially consisted of objecting to the cruelty of her aunt and cousins, and insisting on telling the truth. The headmaster of the institution where she was sent to school singled her out to the other girls as a liar, made her stand on a stool for hours to think about her wickedness, and told the other pupils to avoid her company. In this case, humiliation and isolation were used as a punishment, but corporal punishment was also very common through the nineteenth and well into the twentieth century, as it was thought to build character. In fact, it is only recently that corporal punishment has been outlawed in the UK. First, in 1948 the use of the birch was outlawed, and then any form of corporal punishment was banned in schools in 1986. Independent schools only came under this law in 1998. Parents do not come under this law, being allowed to use it as a form of 'reasonable chastisement'.

By the 1970s, when British law stated that all children were entitled to an education whatever their needs and abilities, difficult or antisocial behaviour was often seen as a type of illness or disease and was discussed and treated by professionals such as doctors, psychiatrists and psychologists, rather than teachers. The general opinion then was that the teacher's role was to teach, and that such behaviour was beyond the teacher's knowledge and training. And of course, that last part was true – teachers were not equipped to deal with difficult behaviours, and even today many teachers feel that some difficult behaviours are beyond their training and ability to deal with, and that they should be getting on with teaching rather than being a social worker or therapist.

Let's think for a moment about your personal philosophy regarding children's behaviour and the responsibilities of teachers and TAs in this regard. Complete the sentences on the next page, to express your views on how you believe we should approach behaviour management in schools.

I believe that children's behaviour should be . . .

_____

_____

_____

_____

I believe that teachers and TAs have the following responsibilities in relation to children's behaviour:

_____

_____

_____

_____

If you had to express your ideas about managing children's behaviour in terms of basic principles, what would they be? What part do these principles play in behaviour management? (See Figure 1.1)

- fairness or equity
- children's rights
- freedom of expression
- democracy
- justice
- equality.

Use Figure 1.2 to list three principles that you think are most important in considering children's behaviour, and map some of the implications of those principles.

For example, if fairness is one of the principles that you feel should govern behaviour, the implications may include those shown in Figure 1.1.

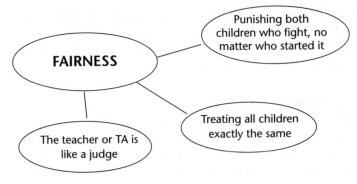

Figure 1.1. Fairness as a principle that guides behaviour management

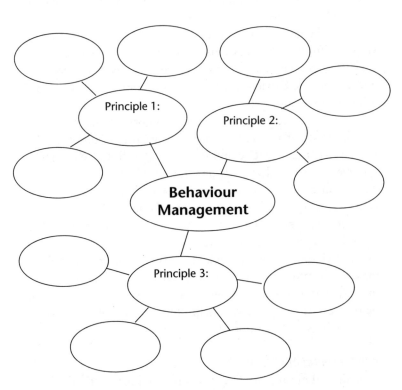

Figure 1.2. Mapping the principles of behaviour management and their
implications

Several major theories have prevailed at different times, based on the thinking of experts who have spent years studying behaviour. See how your thoughts on behaviour align with the thinking of theorists.

A psychodynamic approach

A psychodynamic approach to understanding behaviour is based on the idea that all behaviour is prompted by our unconscious mind, and the internal pressures and drives we all possess, but may not be aware of. This approach has close links to psychoanalysis and the work of people such as Freud in the late-nineteenth and early twentieth century. Because of these links, it tends to focus on decreasing or eradicating inappropriate behaviour. It is a perspective that is not seen as being very helpful in schools because most of the strategies that are suggested for changing behaviour require specialist therapy and cannot be carried out in the classroom by teachers and TAs. Many people are also of the opinion that the reason for inappropriate behaviour is less important than how we manage that behaviour, particularly as we often cannot change or remove the negative influence on the child. We cannot remove neglect or divorce from children's lives, or the distress, anger and guilt that these can produce in children and adolescents. This approach sees poor behaviour as the result of a conflict between inner drives and external demands. For schools, the most practical types of strategies suggested by a psychodynamic approach relate to the recommendations it makes for physical exercise and creative activities (music, drama, pottery) which allow for freedom of expression and 'letting off steam' that can help children act out or portray their feelings and emotions in appropriate ways.

A behavioural approach

Behavioural approaches are based on the premise that human behaviour is a response to stimuli – an event, something that someone else says, the weather, or other elements of the environment. Thus the behavioural psychologist would account for children's behaviour in the classroom by describing it in terms of response to stimuli – what the teacher says and does, the nature of the classroom surroundings, the actions of the other children. Misbehaviour occurs either because the child has not learned to respond appropriately to a particular stimulus (and therefore must be taught better ways of responding), or that the stimulus was poor or inappropriate (for example, the teacher asked a question that confused the child, or the child was not given the proper materials to complete an assigned task). So, according to this approach, if an adult asks a child to do something (stimulus) and the child refuses, he or she needs to be taught the more appropriate response of accepting instruction from adults or responding positively to requests. Examples of poor stimuli might be:

- Unclear instructions or rules, which the child does not understand and therefore apparently 'disobeys'.
- The materials that the child needs to complete a task are not available.
- The child has to work in a space that is too crowded.

The phrase 'ABCs of behaviour' is most often associated with a behavioural approach, and the next chapter will look at Antecedents, Behaviours and Consequences (ABCs) at some length, because it is undeniable that our actions largely consist of responses to people and events, and that there are always consequences to our behaviour. A behavioural approach has had a bit of a bad reputation over the years, however, because of its association with research into the behaviour of pigeons or rats, which can be trained to respond in particular ways to particular stimuli. Critics of this theory say that pupils are not animals who need to be trained to 'jump through hoops' but thinking beings who need to be helped to understand their own behaviour and take some responsibility for it.

A cognitive behavioural approach

A cognitive behavioural approach – in response to criticisms of a strictly behavioural approach – acknowledges that human beings respond to stimuli in the environment, but also tries to engage pupils in thinking about their behaviour and reflecting on possible alternative reactions or responses to stimuli. According to this approach, changing behaviour is not just a case of changing a stimulus or training a child to respond differently, but also of acknowledging and changing the thinking process that goes on behind the response to the stimulus. It is sometimes called a social skills approach, as the behaviours that pupils need to learn are essentially social skills. Teachers who adopt a cognitive behavioural approach talk to their pupils about why they behave in certain ways (especially questioning inappropriate behaviour) and engage pupils in actively changing their own behaviours by generating alternatives, and carefully monitoring how successful they are in choosing the better alternatives when the next opportunity to misbehave occurs. At its most intense, this type of approach is used most extensively with pupils with special needs (largely social, emotional and behavioural disorders – SEBD), particularly as close monitoring of a pupil's behaviour can be very time-consuming and labour intensive for a teacher. However, to a large extent schools and teachers in this country now use a cognitive behavioural approach to managing behaviour.

None of these approaches is either right or wrong – they are just different perspectives on what motivates or prompts the behaviours that children and adults display under different sets of circumstances.

Factors which influence behaviour

'Take no notice – he's only looking for attention.'
'She's just at that awkward age.'
'Why are they always so fidgety on a windy day?'

'Her mother said the rabbit died over the weekend so if she's a bit tearful that'll be why.'
'They've been to their Dad's for the weekend and his new wife's just had a baby.'

These are all typical exchanges about pupils that you might hear between teachers and other adults in schools, particularly during the primary years. But why are these types of information so important? Are we being too intrusive – too nosey about children's private lives? Are we being dismissive or judgemental? These types of statements suggest that we know a lot about children's behaviour and the factors that influence it. List some of the factors suggested by these comments or any others that you are aware of that influence children's behaviour.

_____

_____

_____

_____

_____

_____

_____

Factors which influence children's behaviour

age	physical health	family circumstances
gender	surroundings	emotional wellbeing
culture	self-esteem	current events

Children's behaviour is influenced by a whole cocktail of factors. The same is true of adults. Behaviour is strongly influenced by:

- personal physical factors (how well we feel, how fit we are, whether we are able to do the tasks we need to do)
- our family and social circumstances (how well we get on with family members, whether we left the house on a positive or negative note this morning, whether we feel loved and supported by family and friends)
- external physical factors (the weather, how well provided we are for basic physical needs such as housing and food, the possible stresses of stretched finances).

In the 1940s, the psychologist Abraham Maslow developed what has come to be known as Maslow's Hierarchy – a pyramid of needs that everyone feels (adults and children), and that must be satisfied for us to thrive (Figure 1.3). Interestingly, Maslow developed this theory by studying successful and exemplary people, rather than those who were obviously 'needy,' disabled or unsuccessful in some way. At the base of the pyramid are the most basic physical needs such as food and warmth. Babies operate at this very basic level and they can be very vocal and good at communicating their needs to the adults around them! However, babies also thrive better if they live in an environment where they feel safe and have affectionate carers. We all have these needs, and exactly where we are on Maslow's hierarchy differs according to our current situation – according to whether we are comfortable in that situation or not. Young people and adults are more likely to feel fulfilled and happy if they know their very basic needs are met, they feel loved and a sense of belonging (to family, among peers and in school) and if they have a growing sense of self-esteem as they gain mastery and competence. As a TA, you influence the extent to which these needs are met for the pupils you work with.

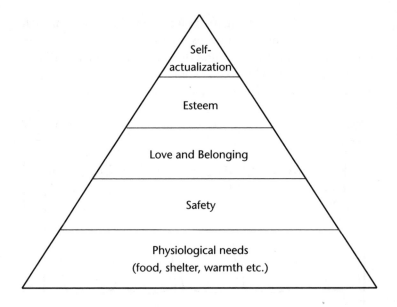

Figure 1.3. Maslow's Hierarchy of Needs

What is acceptable behaviour?

We have used a variety of words so far to talk about behaviour – good and bad/poor, appropriate and inappropriate. Although we may categorize the behaviours which we see in school in these ways, and may even describe individual pupils as well behaved or badly behaved, in reality behaviour is rarely seen in such black and white terms, behaviours vary in intensity and seriousness, and most children are sometimes well behaved and sometimes not.

Behaviour on a continuum

Think of the different behaviours that you see from pupils during the course of your working day – those that are good or bad, appropriate or inappropriate. Use the picture of the washing line to show which *classroom* behaviours you would find totally acceptable or totally unacceptable, or somewhere in between. (If you want to 'practise' or think this through before you commit your ideas to the page, you can write behaviours on Post-it notes and then re-arrange them until you are satisfied with where you would place them on the line.) There are already a few examples to give you a good start.

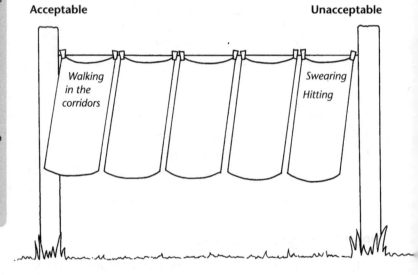

Acceptable   **Unacceptable**

Walking in the corridors

Swearing

Hitting

Figure 1.4. Behaviours I see during my working day:
Are they acceptable or unacceptable?

You have just listed behaviours according to whether they are acceptable in the classroom. But what if you were considering playground behaviour, or behaviour on a field trip? Would you need to move some of the behaviours to a different part of the washing line? Almost certainly you would, because to a large extent the degree to which any given behaviour is acceptable depends on the context in which it happens.

■ Running around is totally acceptable in the playground or during games. We encourage it so that children expend the physical energy that might otherwise prevent them from sitting still long enough to apply themselves to learning, but it would be totally unacceptable in the classroom.

- Sitting still and talking to no one is definitely acceptable behaviour when children are taking exams, but if you saw it happen on a regular basis in the playground, you might be concerned about the pupil's ability to socialize and make friends.

If you work in more than one type of context (classroom support as well as playground or lunchtime supervision) it is important for you to make these distinctions clear. And even within a setting, behaviours would be categorized as acceptable or unacceptable according to the activity that children are engaged in. We will talk more about this in a later chapter on setting expectations. But, take a moment to make a note here – or mark the items on your washing line – of behaviours that are NEVER acceptable, as well as those that are ALWAYS acceptable.

These behaviours are always acceptable in school:

_____

_____

_____

_____

These behaviours are never acceptable in school:

_____

_____

_____

_____

There is a point at which we draw a line – there are some absolutes in terms of behaviour. One of the behaviours that is often found in schools but that is always considered unacceptable is bullying. We will talk about this particular behaviour more in a later chapter, but in the self-evaluation exercise at the end of this chapter you will be asked to start thinking about bullying and what your responsibilities are as a TA if you come across instances of it.

What about pupils with special needs?

Now let's think of another context for behaviour – a classroom for children with special needs. If you have worked in a special school, specialist teaching facility (STF) or pupil referral unit (PRU) you will know that classrooms there generally have quite a different feel to classrooms in ordinary primary and secondary schools.

- In special school classrooms, many of the pupils will be working pre-Key Stage 1 – not just on pre-number work or pre-reading skills, but on what are known as P-scales (which deal with very basic skills such as focusing on an object, or reacting in any way to a person or event). The behaviours that are displayed differ because many children in special schools have physical impairments that limit their mobility and independence, or their speech so that they can only vocalize – that is they have a range of sounds but may not be able to pronounce words or produce structured sentences in order to communicate.

- In STFs, pupils' cognitive difficulties are less severe than in special schools, but some of the behaviours that are common are the result of the difficulties that the pupils have already experienced. A child who is referred to an STF is already behind his or her peers in development and knowledge, has already had to learn to compensate for his or her difficulties, and has already experienced failure in the ordinary classroom. These factors can produce quite negative behaviours until the child begins to succeed due to the additional support that the STF offers.

■ In PRUs, which are specifically designed to support pupils with behaviour difficulties, the range of typical behaviours will also be quite different from those seen in a mainstream classroom, as these are children whose behaviour has been so unacceptable that a mainstream setting is no longer considered suitable. Their behaviour will have seriously interfered with learning, and will continue to do so, until a balance is achieved – that is, until they can begin to experience the success which will motivate them to want to learn, which in turn will help to control their behaviour. However, this is typically not a simple or swift process.

Children with special needs often exhibit a range of behaviours that are closely connected with their disability or particular condition. Some categories of special needs are of course based on behaviours – SEBD is the most obvious example – but children on the autistic spectrum (including those with Asperger's syndrome), with Down syndrome or Tourette's syndrome often display behaviours that we would consider unacceptable in a mainstream classroom but that stem largely from their disability. And, of course, with the trend towards mainstreaming in the last 20 years or so, many of these children are placed in ordinary schools and mainstream classrooms.

How do you see children with special needs in terms of behaviour management? Can we apply the same standards to their behaviour as we do to the behaviour of other children? Do you think they should abide by the same rules as other children in the class? Or do you think that they should be exempt from keeping class rules? Should we apply the same consequences to their inappropriate behaviour as we do to any inappropriate behaviour? Take a moment to write your thoughts about the extent to which you think children with special needs should be required to obey the same rules as other children.

What about cultural differences?

Many years ago as a relatively new teacher I went to work in central London, and for the first time was surrounded by children from a whole range of nationalities and cultures. Unfortunately I knew very little about most of those cultures and misinterpreted many of the behaviours that I saw in these children, until I learned to better understand them. More recently I worked in the United States and had several opportunities to work with Native American teachers and TAs on the Indian reservations, which presented me with a whole new cultural set. This is not a group that you are likely to encounter in your work, but it does provide a type of case study for considering how culture affects our expectations of behaviour and how we interact with other individuals.

> The Navajo Indians in the south-western United States have a culture of cooperativeness, and working for the good of the group rather than seeking or promoting individual interests. This includes a general respect for other people and their opinions, so that when Navajos speak – in a group or with another individual – they

never interrupt, and even wait a while before taking their turn to speak, to make sure the other person has finished what they have to say. Their conversations are made up of silences as well as speech. They also tend to speak quietly, not raising their voices, and will generally keep their eyes averted rather than making constant eye contact. In what might seem to be quite a contrast, Navajos will often borrow and use other people's belongings without asking. They generally do this – with every intention of returning them in good condition when they have finished with them – on the basis that if the owner is not currently using an item, they see no reason why they should not make use of it themselves.

You may also be interested to know that most teachers in Indian reservation schools are not Native Americans. So what implications do you see for behaviour management in these cultural norms of the Navajo? How might they affect interactions between teachers and pupils or teachers and parents?

_____

_____

_____

_____

_____

_____

_____

The Navajo way of life may sound like the ideal of our version of democracy, but in practical terms it means that:

- Navajo children are taught to be non-competitive, and we do typically use competition to motivate our pupils. We have team games, and we celebrate individual achievement – not only in athletics but also in spelling tests and even attendance at school. A Navajo child will hinder his or her own progress to help another Navajo along. To consider yourself better than someone else is not in their vocabulary or culture.

- Conversations may seem stilted and unnatural, but perhaps more importantly, a child may appear unwilling to respond to an adult's question, as he waits respectfully to make sure the adult has nothing more to say, and he may even seem quietly defiant as he stands silent with eyes averted.

- Class discussions lack the energy and enthusiasm we hope for, as pupils learn to express their opinions openly and confidently, and respectfully but boldly challenge the opinions of others in the class.

- Children may be accused of stealing, with all that that implies for our belief in their general trustworthiness and their relationships with other pupils.

There is only a very slim chance that you will ever teach a Navajo child, but it does serve as a reminder that whenever we interact with children from a different cultural background to our own, their perspective will always differ from ours in some way.

There are many books about behaviour management and most of them include sections on special needs and cultural differences, so there is a wealth of material available for you to research in greater detail. However, here are a few basic principles:

- You have responsibility for the behaviour of all the children you work with – and that includes children with special needs and those from other cultures.

- All children can learn to behave appropriately, given the right motivation and support. Their motivations may differ and expectations may be different, but your basic expectation must be that you can and will work with them.
- When you encounter unacceptable behaviour, remember that it has been learned and may even have been taught to the child by a responsible adult, as their version of acceptable, respectful behaviour.
- Be better informed. There are too many myths about children with special needs, and we often know too little about the different cultural backgrounds of our pupils. The more you understand, the better equipped you will be to help manage all children's behaviour with confidence. Read. Talk to your supervising teacher. Ask colleagues who work with children with special needs.

Chapter summary

In this chapter we have looked at some of the different philosophies that drive behaviour management, and you have had an opportunity to consider your own personal philosophy, or beliefs about children's behaviour and the responsibilities you feel that teachers and TAs have for managing children's behaviour. There are many different influences operating on children's lives, and these all combine to affect their behaviour in both positive and negative ways. You have also had a chance to consider what constitutes acceptable behaviour – in the classroom and other school settings – and the sort of behaviours, such as bullying, that can never be considered acceptable. We have also briefly looked at two areas of particular concern for behaviour management – special needs and cultural differences – and the extent to which you might modify your expectations for pupils who come from different cultural backgrounds or who have special needs. As a TA you may experience some frustration over the negative influences that your pupils are subjected to, but you have to accept that you can work only within a certain sphere – the classroom and to a certain extent the wider school environment. However, your influence here can be quite considerable, as we will discuss in the later chapters of the book.

Self-evaluation

 Think of the children you teach who come from a different cultural background than the majority of the class or school. What differences (if any) do you see in their behaviour?

_____

_____

_____

_____

_____

What allowances do you make (or do you feel you should make) – in terms of behavioural expectations – for these cultural differences?

_____

_____

_____

_____

_____

_____

Think of the children with special needs who you are assigned to work with, or who are in classrooms where you work. What differences do you see in their behaviour?

_____

_____

_____

_____

_____

_____

What allowances do you make (or do you feel you should make) – in terms of behavioural expectations – for these children's special needs?

_____

_____

_____

_____

_____

_____

In a later chapter we will talk more about school behaviour policies, but as a preparation for that, see if you can get hold of a copy of your school's behaviour policy, and take a first look at it.

Tick the box beside each item once you have completed it.

❑ I've tracked down the school behaviour policy and had a quick read. These are my responsibilities for behaviour management in the school according to the school policy:

_____

_____

_____

_____

_____

_____

❑ I've read the section on bullying in the school behaviour policy. These are my responsibilities when I see bullying occurring around the school:

_____

_____

_____

_____

_____

_____

In light of what I've read in this chapter, I've reconsidered my philosophy of children's behaviour and adult responsibilities for managing that behaviour, and come to the conclusion that (tick one of the following):

❑ My perspective and philosophy remain the same.

❑ My philosophy basically hasn't changed but there are some things that I hadn't considered, such as:

_____

_____

_____

_____

_____

❑ Perhaps I need to rethink my approach, in particular with respect to:

_____

_____

_____

_____

_____

The ABCs of behaviour

In this chapter we look at what are often called the ABCs of behaviour: that is, the Antecedents (or triggers) that lead to Behaviour and the Consequences that follow. This particular view – as we discussed in the previous chapter – stems from a behavioural approach, where our actions and reactions are seen as responses to stimuli in the environment. These stimuli originate from external physical conditions, internal feelings and motivations, or interactions with other people. Whatever their source, they form part of a chain of behaviour and consequences which can have either a negative or a positive outcome in the classroom. We spend a whole chapter on this topic, because as a TA you can modify or help to eliminate certain stimuli which lead to negative outcomes in the classroom, and increase the occurrence of stimuli which lead to positive outcomes. Learning to recognize antecedents or triggers to appropriate and inappropriate behaviour is the first step in this process. It is also helpful to have a greater awareness of the consequences that naturally occur, and those which you may impose. It really does make sense to know your ABCs!

Antecedent $\longrightarrow$ Behaviour $\longrightarrow$ Consequence

Antecedents – What happens to trigger behaviour?

Almost anything that happens in the classroom could be seen as a potential antecedent. What you say or do, what any of the pupils say or do, noises, someone coming in with a message, a change in activity – these all trigger or prompt different sorts of behaviour. Let's take a minute to think about some of the things you see children do, starting with some of the most common negative behaviours, and think about possible antecedents. List three or four of these in the table and then list what you think typically triggers them. It would be useful if you could think of more than one possible trigger for each example, but think in terms of the simplest antecedents rather than larger happenings such as family dynamics or life-changing events. The table has an example to start you off:

If a child . . . (behaviour)	the antecedent or trigger might be . . .
hits another child	the other child said something insulting to them, or the other child hit or poked them first, or the other child interfered with their work or belongings

Table 2.1. Possible antecedents for common negative behaviours

Often when we challenge a child about an inappropriate behaviour, they say, 'He hit me first!' or 'She said bad things about my mum!' Without realizing it, they are identifying the antecedent for their behaviour. The suffix 'ante' means 'before' – as in the words antenatal and antediluvian – and children can tell you that something came before (and as they would claim, caused) their inappropriate behaviour. We may not think they are justified in reacting the way they did – and we will say more about this in a moment – but they are right in recognizing the chain of events. Their behaviour was prompted or triggered by something that happened first. As they would claim, 'He started it!'

It is very easy to think of antecedents for negative, challenging behaviours but there are also antecedents for the positive and appropriate behaviours that you see in your classroom. So take a moment to think of some of the good things you like to see happening, and what might have triggered those behaviours. Use the next table; it gives an example of a positive behaviour to start you off.

If a child . . . gets their work done as requested	the antecedent or trigger might be . . .
_____	_____
_____	_____
_____	_____
_____	_____
_____	_____
_____	_____

Table 2.2. Possible antecedents for common positive behaviours.

You may have found it more difficult to complete this second table. Why does a child complete his or her work properly and promptly?

- It may have been a type of task that he particularly liked, or that he knew he could do well.
- He may have been promised free time or some other reward for finishing quickly.
- He would certainly have to understand what was required of him, and have the necessary skills and equipment.

And likewise for all of the positive behaviours you try to encourage in your pupils – respect, politeness, punctuality, talking only when it is their turn, handing in homework on time, bringing their PE kit and library books on the right day – whether these are academic or social behaviours, a variety of antecedents may prompt them.

Did you notice much difference between the type of antecedents you recorded in the first table, and those that you just recorded in the second table? Quite apart from the antecedents which we have no control over (such as the weather or even the timetabled activity), two things usually emerge from this sort of exercise:

1. The triggers to negative behaviours are usually also negative. They may not be serious examples of misbehaviour – just one child giving another the odd poke or mild insult, or taking something without asking – but they are the sort of thing you would generally discourage. The triggers for positive behaviours are usually positive.
2. The antecedents for negative behaviours are often tangible, physical occurrences (hitting, kicking, verbal taunts), whereas the triggers for positive behaviours are more often internal and emotional. They relate to motivation and enjoyment, even anticipation of a positive outcome (such as praise or free time).

Do you see an apparent contradiction here? We have said that one of the antecedents for positive behaviour may be the consequence that follows (or that the child is anticipating will follow).

A	B	C
Anticipated/ promised reward	Child completes his work	Receives a reward

So although an antecedent is by definition something that precedes a behaviour, that antecedent can be the reward that will follow the desired behaviour. The promise that precedes the action acts as a trigger. Even if you have made no specific promise of a reward, if the pupil has good reason to believe he will receive some sort of reward, because it has happened before as a consequence of similar good behaviour, this may also be sufficient to trigger the good behaviour. Bear this point in mind – it will come up again as we talk about rewards and sanctions in Chapter 4.

This situation also highlights another point which we will return to later in the book – the difference between intrinsic and extrinsic motivation. We offer positive consequences such as points, praise or free time to our pupils to encourage them to behave appropriately. These are external rewards, or extrinsic motivation. What we really want, and should be working towards, is for pupils to be self-motivated and to behave appropriately because they gain satisfaction from it. They work hard and complete their assignments, and that gives them a sense of satisfaction. Moreover they see that they are increasing in knowledge and skills – they are seeing the success that stems from hard work. This is intrinsic motivation – it comes from within. It is the feeling you get when you see that wonderfully neat cupboard or your car gleaming in the driveway – made that way by your efforts. Even if sorting a cupboard or washing a car is not your favourite occupation, it gives you pleasure to see the results, and that is why you do it

– not because someone is going to come along and give you a gold star.

Behaviour – Is it a question of choice?

One of the things that we try to teach children and teenagers about their behaviour is that they almost always have a choice, and that they should learn to exercise that choice. They do not always have to react to what other people say or do – they can be proactive and decide or act for themselves. The Department for Education and Skills (DfES) induction training for TAs in England emphasizes the importance of using the 'language of choice' in the unit on promoting positive behaviour (there are instructions for how to access these materials in the appendix). It is a real sign of maturity when children and teenagers take on this concept and you can see the beneficial effects on their interactions with adults and other pupils. And we do teach it from a very early age.

Think of an example of 'choosing your own behaviour' that we might teach a nursery-age child? Even if you do not teach this age group, you could consider examples from interactions with nieces and nephews or other young children.

We tell nursery-age children not to hit, even if someone hits them. Hitting back is an instinctive reaction for them, but essentially we are trying to instil in them the idea that they are not forced to do it. This is the nursery-level version of 'violence begets violence', and it begins the process of teaching them that they can – and should – play their part in stopping the cycle. We teach these principles early on and continue to try and instil them into children throughout their school years.

What about secondary school children? Can you think of an example of what we might try to teach children of this age in relation to choosing their own behaviour rather than always reacting to other people's actions?

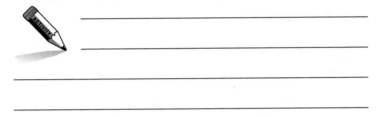

At secondary level we are often teaching teenagers to look beyond their immediate surroundings and consider their actions in the light of longer-term consequences for themselves, or the effects that their behaviour has on a wider group such as their family or community. Some teenagers arrive at secondary school without having grasped the most basic level of this concept that we teach in nursery school. They continue to react to others rather than making a considered choice. Teenagers who lack these skills always get themselves in trouble, but will usually blame other people for it.

So to the child who says, 'He made me do it!' we say: No one can make you do anything you don't want to. Although this is not true in all aspects of a child's life, because it is part of childhood to be under the influence of adults who make decisions and shape children's behaviour, the principle remains that they can be active choosers of how they behave in many instances. In a later chapter we will talk more about this principle of behaviour as a choice, when we discuss the ABCs of adult behaviour and how we adults can also learn to be proactive rather than always reacting to what other people (especially our pupils) say and do. This really is a question of self-discipline and self-control – of real autonomy in their young lives.

Consequences – good and bad

Consequences. How would you define the word? Take a minute to write your personal definition and some examples of consequences.

 I would define a consequence as

_____

_____

_____

Some examples of consequences:

1. _____

_____

2. _____

_____

3. _____

_____

4. _____

_____

5. _____

_____

The *Collins English Dictionary* defines a consequence as 'a result or effect of some previous occurrence'.

It comes from a Latin word – *consequi* – meaning to pursue or follow after. We may think of consequences primarily as something undesirable. In fact we often talk about taking or suffering the consequences, as if consequences are never something that we might enjoy. In reality, consequences can be either positive or negative.

> We turn up for work every day . . . and we get paid at the end of the month.
> We get caught by a speed camera . . . and we have to pay a fine.

And in our busy modern lives, there are many things that happen that we really do not think of as consequences, but they are in fact the result of deliberate choices we make:

> We get to the cash desk at the supermarket . . . and we have to pay for the food we've put in our trolley.

We may be shocked by the total, but we are not surprised that we have to pay. After all, we filled up the trolley with goods that we knew would have to be paid for.

> We drive the car . . . and have to fill the tank when it's empty.

Again, we may rant about the rising costs of petrol, but we do accept that choosing to drive, we have also chosen the need to buy fuel.

In a classroom context there are two common synonyms for consequences: rewards and sanctions, or in other words desirable and undesirable consequences. This links to class rules which we will discuss in greater detail in a later chapter, but what is important to note here is the notion of consequences being both positive and negative. It is very important to bear this in mind in all of your interactions, with pupils and other staff, and most certainly comes into effect when we teach children rules and routines for their behaviour in the class-room and around the school.

There is also a question of time scale with consequences. Some consequences are instantaneous – a child completes a task and gets a sticker or points – but some occur with a short time lapse – for example, Golden Time at the end of the week. These types of consequences are usually imposed by adults. And the younger the child, the more instantaneous the conse-quence must be in order to be effective as a modifier of behav-iour. The more natural, longer-term consequences are the ones that we cannot impose. If a child never finishes an exercise in class or a homework assignment, the chance of long-term academic success (passing GCSEs or A levels, getting into college or university, getting an apprenticeship or other voca-tional placement, and eventually a satisfying job) becomes lower. These are the things that we may threaten children with when they refuse to do homework or apply themselves to coursework, but as motivators they are practically useless. Children in primary school cannot see the relationship between getting 10 out of 10 in a spelling test this week, and

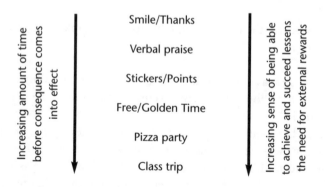

Figure 2.1. Short-, medium- and long-term consequences

realizing their dream of becoming or fireman or a rock star in ten or fifteen years' time. And teenagers, who have a better theoretical grasp of time and cause-and-effect, are generally too self-absorbed to make the leap, or consider it more important than the latest computer game or fashion statement.

Chains of ABCs

Let's look at some examples of the ABCs as they occur in class.

Imagine Dan, sitting at his desk.
Dan hits John (Behaviour)
But . . . John had poked Dan first (Antecedent)

A	B	C
John pokes Dan	Dan hits John	?

What are some of the possible consequences that might follow? List some of them here:

1. _____

2. _____

3. _____

4. _____

5. _____

In a classroom setting the consequences are likely to fit into one of two categories:

- John may hit Dan back – that is, the consequence originates from one of the two people already involved, or
- The teacher or TA might notice Dan hitting John and intervene – that is the consequence is imposed by someone in authority.

There are other possibilities – another child may see the exchange and intervene to smooth things over – particularly if the class has been promised a group reward for good behaviour. Or other children may see what is happening and actually join in, making the situation worse.

These instances of A – B – C are not isolated, but are often continuous and lead on to a whole chain of behaviours and consequences, as one consequence becomes the trigger for a new behaviour, which in turn brings a new consequence into effect. Let's take the example of John and Dan again.

A	B	C
John pokes Dan	Dan hits John	John hits back

A	B	C
John hits back	Dan yells out	TA intervenes

As these are negative behaviours and negative consequences, the chain should be broken as soon as possible, because the longer they last, the more ugly the situation becomes. Tempers rise, and what started as mild insults or jostling can become a feud that carries on during break and lunchtime, and has the boys' parents marching up to the school to find out what is going on.

So it would be much better if the sequence were:

A	B	C
John pokes Dan	Dan hits John	TA intervenes

What form might your intervention take in such a situation? In other words, what do you think might be appropriate consequences here?

_____

_____

_____

_____

We talked earlier about behaviour being a matter of choice. The particular importance of this idea is that when pupils choose their behaviour they are essentially also choosing the associated consequence. This is a connection that many children do not grasp, and perhaps we do not teach it as explicitly as we could. The corollary of this idea is that if there is a desirable consequence, that pupils really want, then they can prompt that consequence by choosing the appropriate behaviour.

A simple, common example is:

'Free time if you get your work finished quickly and early.'

We need to help pupils understand that if they really want free time, they can have it, but the price they pay is to get on with their work and make sure they get it finished. The choice is theirs. But many children do not see the direct connection between their actions and the consequences. They will hotly protest: 'But you said we could have free time!' even though they have not finished their work. They must be taught – step by step, five minutes at a time if necessary, with a timer if it helps – that their behaviour is leading to a particular consequence, and if that is not the one they want, they must change their behaviour. Many pupils who struggle to behave appropriately cannot manage to keep the end in view for more than a few minutes.

American educators will sometimes refer to the Premack principle, or 'Grandma's rule', when talking about consequences. It goes something like this:

> 'You can have your dessert when you've eaten your vegetables.'

There are three things worth noticing here:

1. The offered reward (dessert) is contingent upon the desired behaviour (eating vegetables), so the child knows not to expect dessert unless he or she eats the vegetables.
2. The reward is stated up front, as an enticement – it is much more inviting and children will more likely listen if you talk dessert first and conditions afterwards.
3. The whole principle is stated in positive terms: '*when* you've eaten your vegetables', not '*if* you eat your vegetables'. There's an implicit expectation that the child will eat the vegetables – and will therefore get dessert.

Too often such things are stated as threats:

> 'If you don't eat your vegetables, you're not going to get any dessert!'

A statement such as this implies that we're really not expecting you to eat your vegetables – or get dessert – whereas if it is stated the Premack way, it is as if that is not even a consideration. There is also an implicit expectation in this type of statement that you are probably not going to eat your veg. So the consequences do not look promising either for the child

(C = no dessert) or the adult (C = having to refuse to serve dessert to the child). And what will the subsequent consequence be? You can see that there's trouble brewing!

Assertive discipline

Assertive discipline is an approach to behaviour management that was first proposed by an American husband and wife team, Lee and Marlene Canter, in the mid-1970s. Since then it has been used very widely in American schools, and some of its principles have been adopted by schools in Britain. If you are interested to find out more about assertive discipline, there is a great deal of information on the internet. But of interest to this discussion are two of the basic principles which the Canters proposed:

- Teachers should be able to feel that they are in charge of the classroom, and that they can teach without being interrupted by inappropriate behaviour.
- A firm, consistent approach to behaviour management is in the best interests of all the pupils.

Also, one of the aims of assertive discipline is to help pupils learn to choose appropriate and responsible behaviour for themselves.

Although assertive discipline has sometimes been criticized for being too authoritarian, it is certainly not intended to be that way. It encourages teachers to build strong, positive relationships with their pupils, so that the pupil who misbehaves and has to be 'disciplined' understands that the teacher is disciplining him or her out of concern, not through malice or because the teacher is a control freak. So whether the behaviour and the consequences are positive or negative, the teacher's attitude must always be consistent, firm and caring.

One of the suggestions for behaviour management that is associated with assertive discipline is the idea of having a range of consequences for inappropriate behaviour, increasing in seriousness or intensity if the behaviour persists. It would go something like this:

- Initially, if a child calls out in class when he or she should be working quietly, the teacher/TA's response could just be to ignore it. This may seem like a non-response, but if the child is just looking for attention (and children of all ages can be attention-seeking and will use this basic type of tactic to get attention) he or she needs to understand that there are better ways of getting attention than making a nuisance of themselves and disrupting the class.
- If the behaviour is repeated, then the teacher/TA can make eye contact and perhaps raise an eyebrow or otherwise communicate, 'I hear you – but I don't quite like it.'
- If the behaviour persists, the teacher/TA could call the child over with his or her work – or go over to the child's desk – and ask if the child needs help. If he does, the teacher/TA should help the child, and then send him back to his seat with a reminder of the more appropriate way of getting help if he needs it again – by putting up his hand.

We will re-visit these ideas in Chapter 4 when we talk about supportive discipline.

Chapter summary

In this chapter we have discussed the idea of the ABCs of behaviour – the fact that all behaviour is triggered by something (known as an antecedent), and is followed by a consequence. Any number of things can be antecedents, and as a TA you may have only limited influence over them, but you often can control the consequences of a pupil's behaviour. This applies to both appropriate and inappropriate behaviours. In the case of inappropriate or challenging behaviour, it is particularly important for you to intervene as early as possible, so that the negative behaviour can be stopped as soon as possible. Otherwise the situation can escalate, increasing the likelihood of the poor behaviour continuing and necessitating more serious consequences. Even with appropriate behaviour it is helpful if you take deliberate steps to ensure that positive consequences follow as soon as possible, so that the pupil will feel motivated to repeat the appropriate behaviour. Remember that we said that a positive consequence that has occurred because of a good behaviour can be a powerful antecedent for a reoccurrence of that behaviour. These points will be particularly useful when we discuss rewards and sanctions in Chapter 4.

Self-evaluation

Take some time here to think about some of the behaviours that you typically see in your classroom, and the antecedents and consequences that are associated with them. Use the form on p. 53 to:

1. Identify one typical behaviour.
2. Make a note of what might trigger that behaviour.
3. Note the consequences that generally follow.

If you work in more than one classroom you may find that the consequences for a given behaviour differ according to the classroom, because each teacher has slightly different ways of dealing with disruptions and also different tolerance levels. If this is true, make a note of any differences you see. Then:

4. Give some thought to whether you think the consequences are appropriate – that is, are they helpful in reducing inappropriate behaviour or increasing the chances of appropriate behaviours. Or are they in fact doing the opposite of what you would like them to do.

In the next chapters we will be looking at the ways in which we can prompt and reinforce or reward good behaviours and reduce or discourage negative behaviours, so this exercise gives you a chance to think ahead in preparation for those discussions. And lastly:

5. Try to think of some ways in which you might be able to change the behaviour by removing the antecedent or changing the consequences.

This is not a simple exercise, but there is no one right answer. Use your imagination. Ask yourself: 'What if I . . . ?' to think through what might happen if you changed something in the environment that is triggering poor behaviour, or changed a consequence. If you have any doubts as to whether you should make any of these changes, ask your supervising teacher for advice.

If you prefer you could complete this exercise in relation to the behaviour of one particular child, rather than a group or class of children.

Class/Year Group: _____

Typical behaviour

_____

_____

What's the antecedent?

_____

_____

What are the usual consequences?

_____

_____

Do they seem to work? (Do they stop bad behaviour
or increase good behaviour?)

_____

_____

What could I do about this?

_____

_____

_____

_____

_____

3

Setting expectations for behaviour

The most important proactive measure that teachers and TAs can take towards managing behaviour is to set clear expectations, so that pupils know exactly which behaviours are acceptable and which are unacceptable. This helps to establish patterns of good behaviour, which is the primary purpose of behaviour management. Although it is primarily your supervising teacher's responsibility to set such expectations, as a TA you need to reinforce and support your teacher's decisions, and you can also set ground rules for the times when pupils are working with you. In this chapter we look at the different ways in which schools and teachers set expectations for behaviour, starting with school-wide policies and then focusing in on the classroom. This will include an examination of your own behaviour, the antecedents that pupils and other adults present to trigger it, and the choices you can make about how you behave.

Setting clear expectations for behaviour is like giving pupils a map. It shows them where you want them to go and how they can get there. The destination is Learning, or success in school, and they need to understand that they can succeed in reaching this destination if they carefully follow the instructions which you give them. As in most journeys, there is pleasure and enjoyment to be had along the way – the final destination is not the only aim – but the journey is enhanced and more enjoyable when we know where we are going, and are not constantly being delayed by unnecessary diversions and dead-ends.

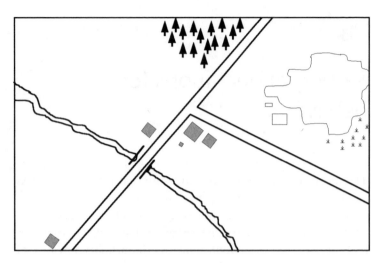

Figure 3.1. The roadmap to learning

Behaviour around the school: What's your school policy?

Somewhere on your school premises there will be a document describing the school's behaviour policy. The 1997 Education Act requires schools to have such a policy, which must be available for school staff, parents and governors to consult whenever they wish. The Elton Report and Lee Canter's assertive discipline, which we referred to in the last chapter, both recommend a whole-school approach to managing behaviour. Hopefully in your school a behaviour or discipline policy is readily available and not gathering dust somewhere on a shelf, or mouldering away in a locked filing cabinet. You can find recommendations for school behaviour policies on a variety of websites, and one of these is listed in the appendix. But first, take a moment to answer these two related questions:

Why is it important for a school to have a behaviour policy? And how might things be different or difficult without a whole-school policy?

I think it is important to have a whole-school behaviour policy because . . .

_____

_____

_____

_____

Without a whole-school policy, I think there would be these differences and potential difficulties:

_____

_____

_____

_____

The 1989 Elton Report strongly stressed the link between learning and behaviour. It also strongly recommended that all schools should have behaviour policies, as a means of establishing a *consistent* approach to behaviour management. This is a major consideration in behaviour management: effectiveness is largely determined by the extent to which there is consistency throughout the school, within each individual classroom, and between the adults who work there together. Pupils need to know that particular behaviours are acceptable or unacceptable, no matter who is supervising them. The 2005 Steer Report also investigated behaviour and discipline in schools, but the title of the report *Learning Behaviour* highlights two important aspects of school life:

1. Behaviour is learned, so by implication it can be taught.
2. The behaviour we want to see in schools is the type that promotes learning, not the type that interferes with it.

If you remember, the Steer Report was based on six core beliefs. The first of these relates to whole-school approaches to behaviour.

> **Steer Report. Core Belief 1:** The quality of learning, teaching and behaviour are inseparable issues, and are the responsibility of all staff.

What this is actually saying is that you – as a TA – are responsible for

- the quality of children's learning
- the quality of your teaching
- the quality of behaviour that is seen in the school.

Those may seem like heavy responsibilities, and they really are. Children come to school to learn, and you are one of the people responsible for ensuring that that happens. But this is good news, because it also means that you can be a powerful, positive influence in the school and in the lives of the children you support. You are one of a team of adults whose joint efforts ensure that children learn, and that includes their learning behaviour.

Your school's policy may have been written some time ago, but typically it should be a document that was developed in consultation with staff, governors, parents and even pupils. You may need to ask your supervising teacher where you can find a copy, but make a point of reading it. The Self-evaluation section at the end of this chapter provides some questions to guide your assessment of the policy.

Behaviour in the classroom: What are your teacher's expectations?

One of the first questions to ask yourself when you are deciding how to approach and deal with pupils' behaviour is: What are my supervising teacher's expectations? Your role as a TA is to support the teacher and the pupil. In the case of behaviour management, you are supporting the teacher by reinforcing and following his or her stated preferences for pupil behaviour; you support the pupils by helping them to act according to the teacher's expectations.

Think for a moment about your supervising teacher's approach to behaviour management. How would you sum up his or her attitude? A strict disciplinarian, or fairly relaxed and lenient? Does he or she remind pupils of how they should behave on a regular basis before problems arise? Or do reminders only come when behaviour is poor? Jot down some of your thoughts as to how you would describe your supervising teacher's attitude and approach to discipline or behaviour management. If you work with several teachers, you may prefer to consider just one of them. Or you may find it interesting to compare their styles if you find them very different.

This is how I would describe my supervising teacher's attitude to behaviour management or discipline:

_____

_____

_____

_____

_____

_____

Where on this continuum would you place the teacher(s) you work with?

| very strict disciplinarian | moderately strict | very relaxed discipline |

Interestingly many teachers who seem very relaxed about discipline and behaviour management have classrooms which run very smoothly with very few discipline problems. Other teachers who may seem to be very 'hot' on discipline may have to deal with a great number of incidents during the course of a school day. Different groups of pupils obviously present different levels of challenge to teachers. However, there are tools that good teachers use to establish good behaviour, which prevent problems arising. This allows teachers to appear more relaxed about discipline, because they have laid good groundwork. We will take a look at three of these tools in particular: routines and rules, effective teaching, and building positive relationships.

Routines and rules

Routines
Every classroom has routines. Some will be explicit and formal, and others will be less well defined and taken for granted. Take for example the school bell.

Most schools have some sort of bell or other sound system to indicate break-times, the beginning and end of classes, etc., and classroom activities are partly regulated by the ringing of the bell.

Another example of a formal routine is the timetable. In secondary schools, where pupils move around the school for different subjects, timetables may be quite individual even for pupils in the same form or class. In primary schools, all of the children in the same class typically follow the same timetable throughout the day, and most of the timetabled activities occur in the same teaching space with the same teacher.

As a TA you may move around with an assigned pupil or be fixed in one classroom; you may move between several classrooms, but you too have a routine that is determined largely by the school bell and by class timetables. Within the limits of the timetable, teachers form their own routines according to the subject matter they are teaching, the type of activity they have planned, and the age and number of pupils involved in the activity.

During a PE or games lesson, there may be 5–10 minutes for warm-up exercises or introducing new skills, 20 minutes for practising skills, and perhaps 10 minutes of less-structured activity, a game of the pupils' choice, or free time on the apparatus.

During a maths or history lesson there may be 5–10 minutes for reviewing previously taught material, say 20 minutes for teaching new concepts, and then time for pupils to practise or apply what's been taught by completing some sort of exercise or assignment.

These sorts of routines are helpful in managing behaviour because they:

- provide structure and make school life more predictable – which makes most children feel more secure, but is particularly important for pupils who have difficulty in managing their own time and energies.
- give a rhythm to teaching and learning – reviewing previously taught material before teaching new material, and then giving pupils a chance to practise with the material, is a good cycle for supporting and facilitating learning. The pattern of warm-up exercises, structured teaching of skills followed by less-structured activities in games and PE lessons makes good use of physical reserves, and helps prevent injuries.

You probably have no influence over the formal routines such as timetables, but within the time scheduled for you to work with pupils you can establish routines and patterns that support pupils' learning and help them to feel comfortable in the learning environment, thus increasing the likelihood of appropriate behaviour.

Transition time

Another aspect of routine that you can facilitate as a TA, that reduces the possibility of inappropriate behaviour, is transition time – the time that is taken up with moving between classes, or between activities in the same class. Not only is valuable teaching time wasted if transitions are handled poorly, but also too many opportunities arise for pupils to get distracted and misbehave. There should be clear routines for such things as:

- what pupils do when they finish their work
- when they leave the mat to start an activity
- when they first come into the classroom from break or lunch.

With clear expectations in place for such times, pupils spend less time hanging around and deciding what to do for themselves, and more time doing what is most important at that moment – getting to where they need to go and starting the next learning activity. Efficient transitions send the message: We're here to learn – let's get on to it!

In the coming weeks, try to be more aware of transition times so that you can take action if necessary. This is well within your sphere of influence when pupils begin and end their work with you:

- Watch how they behave. Do they just mill around until they are told what to do, or are they purposeful and sure of what to do?

- If they seem unsure, check whether they know what they should be doing next and where they should be going, and encourage them – or give them the information they lack.
- When you work with individuals or groups, make sure they know what they should be doing or where they should be going next, before you dismiss them to that next activity.
- Show your appreciation when they arrive or move around promptly.

Examples of transition time

- The beginning and end of lunch or break times
- Changing a reading book
- Moving from a whole-class activity to small group or individual work
- Getting materials or equipment out of desks/trays/cupboards to start a task
- Moving between lessons in secondary school
- Handing out pieces of paper or books
- Moving between the classroom and the hall for assembly, singing time or PE.

Rules

One of the main ways in which teachers state their expectations of pupil behaviour is to set class rules. This is usually done at the beginning of the school year, and – particularly in the primary phase – rules may be established and chosen with the help of pupils, rather than being entirely imposed by the teacher. This gives children a sense of ownership in the rules and more of a sense of responsibility for keeping them. They are also easier to remember if they have been debated and decided upon, rather than delivered tailor-made.

I remember rules such as 'Don't run in the corridor!' and 'No talking in class!' School rules always seemed to have an exclamation mark after them – they rang with a voice of authority, as they were shouted down the corridor or across the dinner hall or playground. What rules do you remember from your school days?

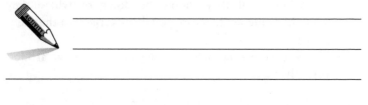

_____

_____

_____

_____

Some things have changed in the last 30 years, but schools and classrooms still have rules. List here the rules that have been set for the classroom where you work. If you work in a primary school, most likely the rules will be on display some-where. This is less likely in a secondary school, so you may have to think more carefully about what the rules are. Think of the things that you hear the teacher repeating to pupils, in order to check or modify their behaviour – the admonitions that are most frequently heard in his or her classroom. If you work in more than one classroom, choose the one where you spend the most time.

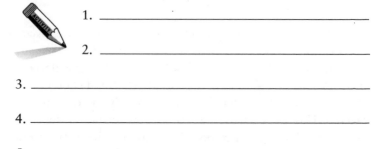

1. _____

2. _____

3. _____

4. _____

5. _____

There are some generally accepted guidelines for 'good' rules:

- Keep them simple, covering one area of behaviour or principle at a time.
- Express them in positive terms, e.g. *Walk in the corridors*, rather than *Don't run*. This puts the focus on promoting positive behaviour rather than repressing negative behaviour.
- Keep the number of class rules down to a maximum of four or five. This will cover most of the important areas, and more than that will be forgotten.
- Display the rules and review them periodically, changing or replacing any that seem irrelevant or unhelpful.

Now look back at the rules that you listed for the class where you work, to see how well they meet the criteria for well-written rules. Would you modify any of them? What changes would you make? Make a note here of any that you feel could be changed for the better and write a better version.

_____

_____

_____

_____

_____

_____

The American classroom management expert Harry Wong, in his book *The First Days of School*, suggests that teachers should spend the first two or three weeks of the school year teaching behavioural expectations – that is, rules and routines – and almost nothing else. He maintains that rules and routines need to be taught and learned like any other school subject. This is in line with the core beliefs of the Steer Report, as was mentioned in the Introduction. However, Harry Wong goes as far as to state that when pupils do not learn rules and routines properly, this seriously interferes with academic progress, like any other poorly learned material. Although mastery of rules and routines is not a basis for learning to read, for example, a child who does not understand how to behave appropriately in class will be hampered in learning to read every bit as much as the child who does not understand that words have meaning and that English is read from left to right. This puts rules and routines into quite a different light – not just peripheral and something that you deal with once at the beginning of the term, but as the Steer Report suggests, integral to learning.

When you teach new knowledge or skills, you give your pupils opportunities to practise and apply them by answering questions, discussing implications or repeating physical movements many times until they are well engrained and understood. In teaching terms this is sometimes known as 'guided practice' because pupils are practising their new skills as you watch them and give feedback on the accuracy of their answers and understanding. You can help pupils to learn appropriate behaviour by asking questions, discussing the implications of keeping or breaking rules and role-playing different scenarios. You can guide them through this process of learning by giving them feedback in these practice situations, so that they will be more competent to use their learning independently.

In the first chapter we talked about acceptable behaviour, and the fact that the definition of what is acceptable changes according to context. Much of what is acceptable and would be encouraged in the playground is not necessarily the sort of behaviour you would want to see inside the school building. You need to make these distinctions clear to your pupils otherwise many of them will not get the message and get into trouble for inappropriate behaviour. It is not a question of children not being able to understand – even young children can appreciate that rules change according to context as they are allowed to run around in the park but not in the car park. It is just a question of being very clear, so that there is no misunderstanding. This is especially important if you work in more than one type of context (classroom support as well as playground or lunchtime supervision).

The behaviours that are considered acceptable must be associated with the context, not with the person in charge. Pupils need to understand that whoever is in charge, the same standard prevails in any given setting – this takes us back to the philosophy of a whole school approach. It is not a question of whether you are prepared to be more tolerant of certain behaviours when you are supervising at playtime rather than working in the classroom. The rules are different, so any adult should be more tolerant. These types of distinctions can be taught systematically through the sort of guided practice that Harry Wong recommends.

How does good teaching affect behaviour?

Steer Report. Core Belief 3: There is no single solution to the problem of poor behaviour but all schools have the potential to raise standards if they are consistent in implementing good practice in learning, teaching and behaviour management.

We all know that if children are so badly behaved that they will not even sit down and listen to the teacher, they will not be able to learn anything in school. However, the other side of this coin is that if children are completely engaged and interested in learning, they will have little time or inclination to misbehave. Good teaching is one of the most effective behaviour management tools in a teacher's repertoire. Why do you think this is so?

In the previous chapter we talked about positive and negative behaviours, and the fact that the consequences of a particular behaviour can be a trigger for a repeat of that behaviour:

- a pupil behaves in an appropriate way (B)
- receives some sort of reward (C)
- that reward (A)
- prompts him to repeat the behaviour (B)
- for which he is also rewarded (C)

This is true of both academic success and social behaviour. We have also already referred to the fact that children and teenagers who are failing at their schoolwork will often misbehave as a distraction, and to draw attention away from their

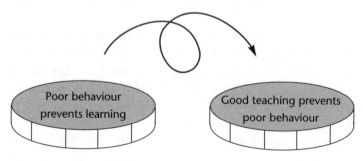

Poor behaviour prevents learning

Good teaching prevents poor behaviour

Figure 3.2. Behaviour and Teaching/Learning: Two sides of the same coin

failures or shortcomings. If they have failed often enough, they have no further interest in even trying to learn, and resort to 'messing about', as a more entertaining pastime. And they become very successful at it. They know how to get a rise out of the teacher, how to annoy other children in the class, how to get sent out of class. Success is a very powerful motivator – even if it is a type of success we would not wish to promote.

Let's go back to the analogy of a map, which we used at the beginning of the chapter. For a minority of pupils who have already experienced too much failure in school, the ultimate destination of Learning seems so remote that they have no motivation to aim for it. If they have already experienced too little success, it recedes beyond their grasp and they give up on it. So much for the intended destination. The journey through school still has to be endured. So they use their creativity and intelligence to make that journey as enjoyable as they can, but instead of channelling it into learning, they create diversions and deliberately take side roads, because this is the only way they can get some pleasure out of school. Success in learning is very motivating. It generates satisfaction, self-esteem and enthusiasm for more learning. Pupils who are successful are not looking to misbehave – they want to engage in the learning process. They want to know more and feel the growing power of increasing knowledge.

Think of the times in the day when the class is most likely to be attentive and fully engaged in learning. What is it about that particular time or activity that produces or encourages pupils to behave so well and to be focused on work rather than being distracted and badly behaved? What are they most likely to be doing?

Now think of the times when your pupils find it most difficult to concentrate on their work and when you find it the most difficult to control their behaviour. What types of activities are they likely to be engaged in at these times? What features of the activity seem to encourage the more difficult behaviour?

As a TA, one of your roles is to support the teacher in establishing and maintaining a positive learning environment, where pupils will enjoy learning and choose to engage in it. There are several aspects to positive learning environments. They include:

- Interesting lessons that are varied and well presented with a good mix of methods.
- Material that is at the right level of difficulty for the pupils' abilities and interests.
- Suitable physical arrangements, so that pupils can see the board or other focus of attention, everyone can move easily around the room, and with materials easily accessible.

Let's look at each one of these, to see how they apply to your work as a TA.

Interesting lessons that are varied and well presented
This is most certainly an area that you have control over when you are working with individuals or small groups. Think about the way you teach and support your pupils. Do you always use the same method of presenting ideas? Or do you try to be creative to catch pupils' imagination and allow for different learning styles? Do you use visuals, sound, stories and

physical objects to convey ideas and concepts? Or do you rely only on written materials? The content of what you teach is probably dictated by your supervising teacher, but you undoubtedly have some freedom to choose your method. You don't have to be a conjuror – constantly pulling surprises out of a hat to keep your audience's attention – but you can make sure that you use some variety to keep pupils excited about learning.

Material that is at the right level of difficulty

Few pupils will persist with lesson material that is just too advanced for them, and even fewer will enjoy lessons that they consider to be too easy or babyish. Again, the selection of material may be in the hands of your supervising teacher, but you can watch for signs of whether it is too difficult or too easy as you use it. Pupils' body language is a good place to start. Do they huff and puff over the work, and slouch or refuse to make eye contact? Do they complain of being tired or unwell, or that the work is boring? These are all indicators that the level of work is inappropriate to their needs and interests. So as you use the teaching materials, try and pace the work so that the pupils can keep up – going back over material and re-teaching if necessary until they understand. And if they do grasp concepts quickly and show that they already understand, move on – try to avoid giving them more of the same questions or exercises just because that is the way you have always done things – or the way things were when you were in school. It will not be motivating for either of you.

Suitable physical arrangements

Think about the layout of the classroom where you work.

1. Draw a quick sketch of the layout in the box on page 72.
2. Label aspects of it that promote a positive learning environment – make notes outside the box and draw arrows to the appropriate feature. For example, you might label a

storage unit as 'Supplies' and add the note 'well organized and accessible'.

3. If there are aspects of the class layout that you feel are NOT helpful or do not meet the criteria, make a note of those in a different colour, for example: 'Desks very close together – not enough space to move around.'

If you work in more than one class or physical space, choose just one of them – or carry out the same analysis on each of them if you prefer.

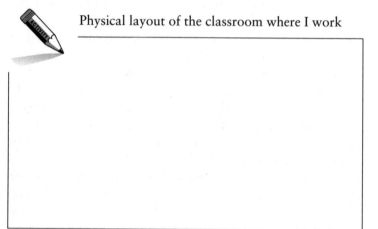

Physical layout of the classroom where I work

Again, as a TA, you probably do not have much control over this aspect of classroom management, but where you see that there are potential problem areas, try to think of possible solutions, and approach your supervising teacher with your suggestions.

The beneficial effects of positive relationships

If you have worked with children or teenagers, you know that a strong relationship is a very good start to being able to manage their behaviour. If we like someone, or generally have a positive relationship with them, we are more willing to do as

Figure 3.3. How do strong relationships promote positive behaviour?

they ask, to consider their preferences, and generally to co-operate with them. Building a good relationship with your pupils begins the very first time you meet, and continues for as long as you associate with them.

What do you do to build good relationships with new pupils at the beginning of the school year? List some of the things that you have found to be helpful over the years. If you are only just beginning your work as a TA, think of the things that have helped to build strong relationships with family members or when you have made new friends.

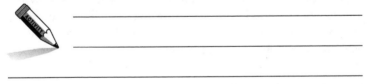

Some of the things we do to build relationships really don't have to take very long. Look at this list of relationship builders that take less than 30 seconds:

▓ A smile.
▓ Saying hello or giving a nod of acknowledgement when you meet.

- Holding the door if the person is coming through behind you.
- Thanking someone for something they have done for you.
- Knowing and using the child's name.

These relationship builders take a little longer, but probably not more than a few minutes:

- Ask questions – and listen to the answers.
- Ask a pupil for his or her opinion – then treat it seriously.
- Stop or sit down to talk, rather than always exchanging comments on the move.

Building positive relationships with your pupils is like money in the bank. Every time you do something to strengthen that relationship, you make a deposit; whenever you do something that spoils the relationship, you make a withdrawal. For pupils with the most challenging behaviour, it can seem a painfully slow process to build a solid relationship, and the slightest difficulty can seem to spoil it, but persistent 'deposits' into the relationship bank will pay off. It makes good sense to build up a good balance in your account for all of your pupils. When the balance is good, you are more likely to have amenable, willing pupils, and the relationship will even be able to weather a few difficult incidents.

The ABCs of adult behaviour

Recognizing what triggers your own behaviours
In the last chapter we talked at some length about the antecedents, or triggers, to pupils' behaviour and the consequences that follow. As one of the adults in the class, it is often your role to 'impose' the consequences of pupil behaviour – giving rewards if it is appropriate, sanctions if it is not. But looked at another way, pupil behaviour is the trigger for the adult behaviour – consequences only happen because another

person is involved and the consequence is inseparable from the person. So the sequence would be:

Antecedent	*Behaviour*
A child misbehaves	You intervene and impose sanctions

This just makes you sound like a neutral agent, but the truth is that many of the behaviours that we see in children act as triggers to our own behaviour in a much more personal sense, at the level of emotions.

Let's think of this chain of antecedent-behaviour relationship in terms of emotions.

When you see a child misbehave, what sort of emotion does that trigger in you?

- Anger?
- Frustration?
- Impatience?
- Exasperation?

Or:

- Loving kindness?
- A desire to help the child?
- Tolerance and compassion?

This is important because our emotions can dictate our actions. If the emotions are negative and we allow them to dictate negative reactions, this will not help the situation, and rarely helps the child to change. We are focusing on possible negative reactions here because those are the ones we want to avoid or eliminate. In a moment we will talk about exercising choice in our behaviour, or how we react to pupils. But the first step is to recognize the triggers. Think of a pupil whose behaviour you find most frustrating and difficult to deal with.

What is it about that pupil that really frustrates you? Make some notes here:

_____

_____

_____

_____

We will return to this list in a moment.

Choosing your own consequences

In the last chapter we talked about behaviour being a choice. We teach children that they have a choice in how they behave, and that in choosing their behaviour they also choose the consequences. So, let's apply this to adult behaviour.

Antecedent	A child misbehaves
Behaviour	You lose your temper because it feels like the hundredth time this week that this child has misbehaved in this way
Consequence	The child answers back, adding to his first offence

And so you build a chain of negative behaviours and increasingly negative consequences. The positive learning environment deteriorates and everyone loses valuable learning time.

This is a simple, negative example, but it is all too easy to get into such a downward spiral. Pupils with inappropriate behaviour do it all the time. As an adult you must take steps to ensure that you do not get caught up in the same type of behaviour. These ABCs become a chain of interactions between you and other people. If it is a chain of negative interactions, you need to break it in some way. Here are some suggestions:

1. Recognize the pupil behaviours that trigger negative responses in you.
2. Tell yourself that such negative behaviours are not aimed at you personally.
3. Determine to stay calm the next time these behaviours occur.
4. Plan what you will say and do next time, rehearsing words and phrases in your mind that you can use.

In a later chapter we will look at these strategies and some of the things you can say and do in more detail. For the moment, just bear this in mind. Life in classrooms is extremely complex, and we rarely deal with single behaviours. We are usually being bombarded by requests from adults and children; we often need to multitask, answering a question while cutting something out or writing something down; and, we may have to juggle several roles during the day (in different classes with different responsibilities, or supervising during lunchtime). These multiple demands on your time can cause quite significant stress, which will magnify the force of triggers to negative behaviour and intensify your reactions and therefore the consequences. In the same way that you teach your children to choose the consequences by choosing their behaviour, take this on for your own behaviour.

In the previous chapter we also talked about the Premack principle or 'Granma's rule': You can have your dessert when you've eaten your vegetables. As an adult you probably use this principle on a fairly regular basis. 'I'll have a cup of coffee when I've washed the car/finished the dishes.' We promise ourselves a treat based on completing a task or achieving something we find difficult. There is no reason why you cannot apply this principle to your work in the classroom. If you are prone to overreact or let your negative feelings dictate your reactions to your pupils' behaviour, then try to be more aware of the triggers and then reward yourself for every morning or day, or even every class period, when you manage to choose a more positive reaction than usual. Do it if you feel it will help you, because it will also help your relationship with your pupils and will help to establish a positive classroom environment.

Chapter summary

This chapter has all been about classroom management, and the many ways in which you can help to establish high expectations of good behaviour in order to create a positive learning environment. This includes physical features such as layout, and the critical element of good teaching. Add positive relationships between adults and pupils – and among the adults who work in the class – and you are well on the way to a working environment which is pleasant and productive for you and the pupils.

Self-evaluation

This self-evaluation exercise looks at two aspects of behaviour management: your school's Behaviour or Discipline Policy, and your own approach to behaviour management for when you are working with groups of pupils or individuals. It is designed to make you more aware of how the school behaviour policy applies to you, and what you do to manage those aspects of the classroom which are under your control.

Part One: Your school's behaviour policy
By now you should have a copy of your school Behaviour or Discipline Policy. Now would be a good time to read it, if you have not already done so. As you read, make a brief note of the following:

- Items that you were not aware of that impact your work as a TA

_____

_____

_____

_____

- Aspects of the policy that are out of your control as a TA

_____

_____

_____

_____

- Anything that particularly surprised you

_____

_____

_____

_____

- Points that you are unsure of – you should clarify these with your supervising teacher

_____

_____

_____

_____

Part Two: Your behaviour management approach

At the beginning of the chapter you thought about your teacher's behaviour management strategies and techniques. We have also looked at some of the recommended ways for establishing your expectations of pupil behaviour. Take some time now to consider what you do when you are working with groups of pupils or individuals to make your expectations clear, and what you might want to change.

1. Are there rules posted in the area where I work?
   Yes / No
2. Do the pupils I work with seem to know what the class rules are?
   Yes / No

Recommendation: If the answer to either of these questions is no, you might want to write out the class rules and put them up where your pupils can see them.

3. How often do I remind my pupils of the class rules? (Daily? Weekly? Rarely?)

   _____

4. When my pupils have problems with behaviour, is it a matter of:
   a. breaking school rules?
   b. breaking class rules?
   c. not knowing routines?
   d. transition times?

Recommendation: Depending on which of these areas you see the problem arising in, go back to the relevant section in the chapter and decide what you can do about it. Consult your supervising teacher if you need help. Write your thoughts about how you can help to improve the situation opposite:

_____

_____

_____

_____

_____

_____

_____

_____

_____

_____

Rewards and sanctions

Discussions of behaviour management are never complete without a discussion of the rewards or incentives that are available to those who behave appropriately – and of course the sanctions that must be imposed for inappropriate behaviour. In the last chapter, we looked at the idea that setting expectations for learning and behaviour is like giving your pupils a roadmap – it shows them where they are going and how they can get there. If we extend this analogy to the rewards and sanctions associated with appropriate and inappropriate behaviour, it adds detail to the map. If pupils follow the directions you give them, they will not only move in the right direction, but the road will be easy. If they fail to follow directions and go off at a tangent, it slows down their progress and diverts them from the desired destination of learning. But it will also get them into a mess – they will figuratively get bogged down in a muddy field or trapped in the brambles – natural consequences of leaving the road, and heading off in the wrong direction.

So in this chapter, we look at

- How you can support your teacher in the incentives that he or she offers to pupils.
- What constitutes a reward, and whether you can give too many of them.

We will also look at different forms of discipline – preventive, supportive and corrective – and see how they fit with what we have already discussed in this book, and what is still to come. In the discussion of corrective discipline you will be asked to consider your role in imposing sanctions on pupils, particularly when they relate to very challenging behaviour.

Supporting your teacher's incentive plan

In the last chapter you noted some of your teacher's behaviour management methods, but this was in quite general terms. So let's be more specific. See if you can answer the following questions about the ways in which your supervising teacher promotes and encourages appropriate behaviour:

1. What incentives does your teacher offer pupils for good behaviour?

    _____

    _____

    _____

2. What types of behaviour earn them these incentives?

    _____

    _____

    _____

3. How often can pupils earn these incentives?

    _____

    _____

    _____

Incentives come in many forms, and a selection is listed in the box. Some are very obviously longer-term incentives, such as end-of-term parties or trips. Others, such as points or tokens, may be available every day, although they may also be cumulative and lead to the larger, longer-term rewards. But which of these incentives or rewards are you empowered to give as a TA?

Incentives take a variety of forms:

house points	stars	smiley faces
tokens	free time	name in a prize draw
merit badges	mention in assembly	end-of-term party

You probably cannot promise parties or pizza; you may not be able to offer free time as an incentive. In fact, your authority to offer rewards may be restricted to the most short-term and small-change versions, as it were. But these can be the most powerful, because they are the most immediate. This is especially true of pupils who have trouble controlling their own behaviour – they cannot sustain the effort needed to earn end-of-term parties and treats. The time scale is too long and therefore unrealistic for them, so they need frequent small rewards to keep their behaviour appropriate. But even well-motivated pupils will respond well to the smaller, instant rewards, and they will appreciate the added incentive if these are cumulative and contribute to larger and longer-term gains.

The setting where you work, and the amount of time you spend working with individual pupils and groups – as well as your supervising teacher's attitudes – will determine the type and magnitude of the incentives you can offer. Whatever level that happens to be, you play a critical role in supporting your supervising teacher as you follow his or her lead, and use the incentive system that he or she has chosen. Pupils are much more interested in fairness and consistency when it comes to rewards than in the actual size of the rewards themselves.

Rewarding acceptable behaviour

What is a reward?

It's Friday evening. You've just finished a busy week at work, and you've got the evening to yourself. What do you do to reward yourself for surviving another week? Do you . . .

- have a long soak in a hot bath?
- change into your glad-rags and go out on the town?
- invite friends round for dinner?
- go for a long quiet walk, ending up at the pub?
- immerse yourself in domestic concerns to give your mind a break from thinking about other people's children?

Any one of these might sound appealing to you – or perhaps none of them do. Any one of them might be considered a reward by someone, but they are all quite different. So what is it that makes them potential rewards? Jot your thoughts down here:

A reward is a reward because . . .

_____

_____

_____

The notion of a reward is entirely subjective. What makes something a reward is the fact that it *appeals to the person it is being offered to*. If you work with different groups of pupils – particularly pupils in different age groups – you may well have found that their idea of what constitutes a reward can differ quite substantially. You must be very alert to what motivates your students, otherwise the rewards you offer will not work – and your pupils will not work for them.

What different sorts of rewards do your pupils respond well to?

_____

_____

_____

In a general sense, a reward is something good that follows from something you have said or done. It is a positive conse-quence. But a reward can also be seen as a prompt or trigger to behaviour as we discussed earlier in Chapter 2. It could be an extrinsic motivator – something offered to a person that encourages them to behave in a certain way – or an intrinsic motivator, where the reward stems from a sense of achieve-ment or satisfaction. In behavioural psychology a reward is seen as reinforcing behaviour – that is, when you give a reward in response to a desirable behaviour, you are making it more likely that that behaviour will occur again. And this is surely why you give rewards to your pupils. You want to send the message: That was good; I'd like to see it happen again.

Behavioural psychologists use the link between behaviour and rewards to devise training programmes for animals – obedience classes for dogs, and training programmes for the dolphins at places such as SeaWorld, for example. Although we like to think of behaviour management in schools as being something less clinical than animal training, the principles are basically the same and there are some interesting hints about rewards that we can adopt from animal trainers. You can read some fascinating stories of animal training in Karen Pryor's book _On Behavior_ (details are in the appendix). She worked for some years as a dolphin trainer. The types of tricks that dolphins perform are really quite complex – they leap through rings high above the water, swim backwards, wave at the audience, etc. How does a trainer get that to happen? Here are three basic principles:

Principle 1: The trainer begins by rewarding very simple actions, such as the dolphin swimming to the end of the pool on hearing the whistle; the dolphin is not expected to perform the final trick immediately, but is trained through the process of building up to it.

Principle 2: The trainer gives rewards for what are sometimes called 'close approximations' of the desired behaviour or action. So if the trainer wants the dolphin to leap out of the water and through a hoop suspended eight feet (2.4 metres) in the air when she blows a whistle, the dolphin is first rewarded for jumping up out of the water; then for jumping up through a low hoop, and then a higher hoop, and so on until eventually the dolphin is clearing the eight-foot hoop.

Principle 3: The dolphin always gets a reward for completing the trick, but that reward is usually just a few small fish – the same reward that has been given all along – the dolphin does not get one fish for each appropriate behaviour at the beginning of the training programme and progress to a tonne of fish by the time he is performing in front of an audience.

In classrooms you are not training dolphins, and although we sometimes use the phrase 'jumping through hoops', it most often denotes mindlessly following instructions. But the comparison with dolphin training is useful. See if you can apply the three principles listed above to your work with children and their behaviour.

Principle 1: _____

_____

_____

Principle 2: _____

_____

_____

Principle 3: _____

_____

_____

We might condense the principles as:

1. Start simply
2. Recognize and support progress
3. It may take a tonne of fish to train a dolphin, but he only gets them one at a time.

Can you give too many rewards?
There is no ideal, magic number for how many rewards you should give your pupils. How many do you think you should give them? How often should you reward good behaviour? Quite simply, good behaviour should be rewarded – in some way – as often as it happens. But here are some guidelines:

- Rewards – or extrinsic motivators – are intended to motivate a child to behave in a particular way (complete a task in a given time, sit quietly when necessary, show respect, etc.). However, they should only be used until the behaviour becomes well established and motivating for the child – that is, the satisfaction of success becomes the intrinsic motivation for the child to continue to behave that way. You can wean pupils off extrinsic motivators by helping them recognize the satisfaction they feel on successfully completing work, or achieving a goal. For example, you can say to a child, 'Doesn't that make you feel good, to finish that essay?'
- Rewards should only be given when they have been earned. How often have you heard an adult promise a child a treat if – and only if – they do a particular thing, and then seen the adult give the treat even though the child has clearly not done what was requested. The adult who

does this is rewarding disobedience. Remember that rewards reinforce behaviour, which makes it more likely to happen again. It is never a good idea to reward disobedience.

- If the reward is verbal praise or a compliment, it must be obvious what the positive comment relates to. Exclamations of 'Well done!' or 'Good boy/girl!' are too vague to be very reinforcing, and can even be misunderstood. Even teenagers need to have things spelled out for them; for younger children this is particularly important.

- The reward should be proportionate to the deed – a small reward for compliance with a small request (Would you pick up those papers, please? – Thank you); larger rewards for compliance with a much larger request or for persistent compliance over time (Homework handed in on time every day earns free time or a choice of activity for part of Friday afternoon).

- Think carefully before you let children choose their own rewards. When, for example, pupils are given a choice of what they would like to do during their free time on a Friday afternoon once they have finished their work, they should be provided with two or three options – all of which are feasible within the time frame – from which they can choose. Otherwise pupils will rightly feel cheated if you give them an open choice and refuse to let them do what they have chosen – even if you are perfectly justified in refusing because it is not a viable option.

When young children come into nursery or Reception class they have to be taught a great deal about how schools and classrooms work – where things belong and the importance of returning things to the right place after use; the routines of the day and the necessity of responding to prompts (such as lining up or returning to class when the bell rings). We praise and reward them as often as possible for following simple routines and instructions. By the time they reach secondary school we expect them to have mastered these basics and be able to operate at a higher level. But there is no harm in continuing to acknowledge the small things that they do well, because these help all classrooms to run more smoothly.

Imposing sanctions

While it is always more pleasant to think of the rewards and incentives that you can give your pupils, inevitably we must give some thought to the sanctions that occasionally have to be imposed in response to inappropriate behaviour. First, however, let's look at three different forms of discipline – preventive, supportive and corrective – and see how they relate to what we have discussed so far.

Preventive, supportive and corrective discipline

Preventive discipline – as the name suggests – consists of all those things which you do to prevent behaviour problems from occurring. They are the proactive measures that we discussed earlier in this chapter and in the previous one:

- The routines and rules that we establish to help pupils know what is expected of them, to give them a greater sense of security, and to make school life more predictable.
- The whole-school policy that establishes a school ethos and philosophy of respect and positive expectations, and provides consistency.
- The rewards you make available to your pupils for appropriate behaviour and hard work.
- The positive relationships you build with your pupils.
- The effective teaching methods that you use to keep pupils engaged in the learning process and productively challenged.

Preventive discipline measures

routines and rules	whole-school policies
clear expectations	promised rewards
positive relationships	effective teaching methods

The Steer Report makes mention of this type of discipline in its core beliefs (see box), and leads us on to supportive and corrective discipline.

Steer Report. Core Belief 2: Poor behaviour cannot be tolerated – it is a denial of the rights of pupils to learn and teachers to teach. To enable learning to take place, preventative action is most effective, but where this fails, schools must have clear, firm and intelligent strategies in place to help pupils manage their behaviour.

Supportive discipline consists of the techniques you use to remind pupils of how they should be behaving, or to nip inappropriate behaviour in the bud. Some examples are listed in the box.

Supportive discipline techniques

- Eye contact
- Facial expressions – a raised eyebrow, or a wry smile, to show the pupil that you know what is going on
- Moving closer to a pupil who is not doing what he or she should (proximity control)
- A physical gesture to re-direct pupils' attention back to their work
- A word of encouragement or reminder

These are the sort of things you do automatically and on a daily basis. They are not punishments or even reprimands. They are just gentle reminders of appropriate behaviour, but they go a long way towards maintaining good discipline because they reduce the minor or budding incidents of inappropriate behaviour. They also show your pupils that you are willing to support them through the process of learning behaviour, rather than immediately reprimanding or punishing them.

Corrective discipline consists of the sanctions that you impose for inappropriate behaviour. When pupils misbehave despite the proactive measures you have taken – that is, despite the preventive measures, and the hints and reminders of supportive discipline – then corrective discipline becomes necessary. It is necessary on several counts:

1. For the good of the misbehaving pupil, because he or she needs to realize that there is a limit to how much inappropriate behaviour can be tolerated.
2. For the good of the rest of the class, as disruptions from one pupil's inappropriate behaviour can prevent them all from learning.
3. To maintain your authority. This is not a question of having undue influence or authority over your pupils, but because you represent the school philosophy at the classroom level, or with the pupils you support. One of your duties as a TA is to help pupils maintain appropriate behaviour.

Corrective discipline is what we often first think of when we see the phrase 'behaviour management', but you will notice that we have spent a long time talking about preventive and supportive measures because they do so much to promote appropriate behaviour and therefore a positive learning environment.

Take a moment now to think of the sanctions that are imposed on pupils in your school who misbehave. Use the graphic to list the various consequences of inappropriate behaviour, depending on how serious it is.

Sanctions

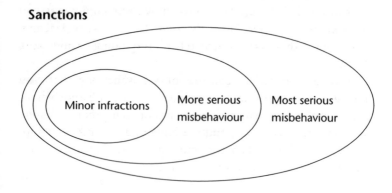

Figure 4.1. Sanctions vary according to the seriousness of the behaviour

The exact sanction which is imposed for a particular behaviour is largely determined by the school where you work. For seriously inappropriate behaviour that is violent or threatening, there are always serious consequences, which may include suspension or exclusion from school. But as with the long-term, larger rewards and incentives that are available to pupils in the school, these types of sanctions are also beyond your jurisdiction as a TA. They are almost certainly beyond the jurisdiction of your supervising teacher. As a TA, the two critical things with regard to sanctions that you need to be clear about are:

1. What sanctions am I allowed to impose, and for which inappropriate behaviours?
2. What should I do when I see behaviours that are inappropriate, but that I know it is outside of my role to deal with?

Your role as a TA is to support the teacher in establishing and maintaining a positive classroom environment, and to support pupils in behaving appropriately. Your ability to do this will be seriously undermined if you try to impose sanctions that you have no power to impose. And for the safety of all the pupils in the school as well as your own wellbeing you must never find yourself in a situation where you do not know who to refer pupils to, or turn to for back-up support if you are faced with seriously challenging behaviour. This type of situation can easily occur if you work with pupils outside the classroom where there is no teacher present, or if you supervise in the playground or during lunchtime. So take a moment to answer these questions. If you cannot answer them with certainty, make sure you consult your supervising teacher and get clarification.

1. What sanctions am I allowed to impose, and for which inappropriate behaviours?

_____

_____

_____

2. What should I do when I see behaviours that are inappropriate, but that I know it is outside of my role to deal with?

_____

_____

_____

The particulars of your role are determined at school and classroom level, but as a general rule when dealing with inappropriate behaviour it is always advisable to use the lowest level of response possible. Then if the behaviour persists, you can increase the intensity of your response. If you immediately impose a harsh punishment or consequence for inappropriate behaviour, there is literally nowhere to go if the behaviour persists. Here is a simple sequence that you can follow:

1. Ignore the behaviour. As long as they are not harmful to the child or others nearby, many inappropriate behaviours can be ignored to begin with. If the pupil is just looking for attention and you ignore him or her, you send the message that behaving inappropriately is not the best way to get your attention. But be sure to give attention for something positive if you can, soon after ignoring the inappropriate behaviour.

2. Provide a subtle hint to let the pupil know that you have noticed the inappropriate behaviour and would like it to stop. This is what you are doing when you raise a finger to your lips to quieten young children. They immediately understand what you mean, and you have not drawn attention to their behaviour or told them off in front of other children. Coupled with a pleasant facial expression, this gives them the benefit of the doubt that they have inadvertently made a noise rather than being deliberately disruptive.

3. Praise good behaviour in another pupil. As a gentle reminder of the behaviour you would like to see, make a point of giving a verbal reward or acknowledgment of the good behaviour in another pupil. This is what is referred to by American teachers as 'praise around'.

4. Teaching interaction. If despite all your attempts to be subtle and supportive the pupil continues to misbehave, this is the time to intervene more deliberately, but you can use your teaching skills rather than wearing the hat of a disciplinarian. Imagine you are correcting a maths problem. If a child used a wrong technique or flawed logic for solving a maths problem, you would point out the error in their working-out, and re-teach the appropriate

method, giving the reason behind the rule or procedure. Do the same thing in relation to the behaviour: simply state the error that has been made, and then state the correct way that the pupil should have followed. There is an example in the box.

> Corrective teaching (maths): You forgot to put in the zero on the second line of this long multiplication. You need to put the zero in, because what we're multiplying here is the tens. And you know that to multiply tens we can just add a zero.
>
> Corrective teaching (behaviour): You took Charlie's pencil without asking. We talked about how you must ask permission before you take someone else's things, otherwise they get cross with you and it starts an argument. So, you need to ask before you take something.

Much of this takes us back to the supportive discipline measures that we mentioned previously, As your response intensifies, notice that the line between supportive and corrective discipline blurs. Even at this teaching stage of the process, however, the correction and sense of reprimand are mild, because you are stating expectations in a positive way and calmly expressing disapproval of the pupil's action. It is not always easy to be so calm and impersonal, so you will find an exercise to help you practise with this technique in the self-evaluation section at the end of the chapter.

A word on bullying

A particularly offensive but all too common behaviour which you may well encounter in schools is bullying. Bullying is any threatening or intimidating behaviour. It may be physical and involve hitting, pinching or jostling, or it may be emotional and involve taunts and verbal threats with no evidence of physical contact. There has even been a growing number of cases of phone or internet bullying with threats being made by one pupil to another via text or email messages. Whichever form it takes, bullying is totally inappropriate behaviour and must not be tolerated in our schools. It almost always happens out of sight of authority figures such as teachers and TAs, and the children who engage in it do so because of their own emotional baggage. Bullying presents a particular instance of a behaviour that you need to know how to respond to. You should be able to answer the following questions:

What is your school's policy on bullying?

_____

_____

_____

What sanctions or punishments are given as a consequence of bullying in your school?

_____

_____

_____

What are your responsibilities as a TA when you see a pupil being bullied by another pupil? What action are you supposed to take if a child reports to you that they are being bullied.

_____

_____

_____

Chapter summary

In this chapter we have looked at some of the ways in which you can reinforce or reward desirable behaviour in your pupils, and how you can respond to pupils who behave inappropriately. As a TA your role is to support your supervising teacher in establishing and maintaining a positive learning environment where pupils know how to behave. You can do this by carefully following your supervisor's lead and providing consistency in rewarding appropriate behaviour and imposing appropriate sanctions for inappropriate behaviour. As you do so, bear in mind the principle that simplest is generally best, and that your first response to inappropriate behaviour should always be low intensity. In the self-evaluation section that follows you will have an opportunity to apply some of the principles we have discussed, and monitor your own success in managing pupil behaviour.

Self-evaluation

There are two parts to this section: an exercise that allows you to track what happens when you use the sequence of low-intensity responses to inappropriate behaviour that was described in the chapter; and an opportunity to develop your repertoire of corrective teaching phrases.

Part I: Using low-intensity responses

First, think of a child you work with whose behaviour is causing you concern. It does not have to be severe behaviour – most of the behaviour that wears teachers and TAs down is of the persistent, mildly irritating sort rather than extremely violent or threatening behaviour. Choose a child you work with regularly.

Now, plan to use the sequence of responses that was described earlier in the chapter with this child, and take note of what happens as you do. Refer back to the appropriate section of the chapter if you need more detail. Briefly the sequence is as follows:

1. Ignore
2. Give a hint
3. Praise other pupils
4. Engage the pupil in a teaching interaction (and see Part II of this section for help with this).

Keep track of what happens as you use each of these levels of response. You may find that you use them all in one lesson, or it may be that you have to use only one or two of them to eliminate the undesirable behaviour, but keep track over the course of several lessons to see if you can detect a change in the pupil's behaviour as you persist in dealing with that behaviour in this low-intensity way. Don't expect instant results. If this is a new tactic on your part, it may take some time for the child to catch on, and for you to get used to using it.

Behaviour causing concern . . .

_____

_____

When I ignored the behaviour . . .

_____

_____

When I dropped hints . . .

_____

_____

When I praised other pupils nearby . . .

_____

_____

When I used a teaching interaction . . .

_____

_____

Part II: Corrective teaching

In the chapter we looked at a sequence of responses that you can use to deal with mild instances of inappropriate behaviour. The final response was corrective teaching – stating clearly 1) what the pupil did that was wrong and 2) what the child should have done. Many pupils who misbehave, when corrected will say with great indignation, 'What did I do?' And they really are not always aware of what they have done. The first step in correcting their behaviour is to help them become more aware of it. Use the table to work up a stock of useful phrases that you can use as corrective teaching statements, as alternatives to merely telling a child what to do or what they have done wrong.

The table on p. 102 gives you some examples to start you off. Add common examples from your own experiences in the empty spaces.

Critical response	Corrective teaching response
Stop talking – please!	You're talking while you're working. Please work quietly.
Stop wandering around the room – sit down!	
Don't shout out the answers.	
Stop kicking the table!	

Table 4.1. Changing responses: From critical to corrective

Helping pupils take responsibility for their own behaviour

In Chapter 1 we talked about the range of behaviours that pupils engage in, and the relative seriousness of those behaviours, according to the pupils' age, abilities, and the context in which they occur. This concept of relative seriousness plays a very important part in the decisions you make about when and how to deal with inappropriate behaviour. So in this chapter you will have an opportunity to consider challenging behaviour and how serious it really is, as well as considering strategies for behaviour change, and looking at how you can motivate pupils to control and shape their own behaviour.

This is a good point at which to remind ourselves that all that you do as a TA should be done under the supervision of a professional. Many decisions about children's behaviour are not yours to make, but should be taken by your supervising teacher. What this chapter will do is give you some tools that will enable you to give more effective support in the classroom. Make sure you understand the extent of your authority and responsibility for behaviour management, so that you know when you can take action yourself to correct behaviour, and when you need to involve your supervisor.

Bad behaviour: How bad does it have to be?

To answer this larger question – how bad behaviour must be before you intervene – we will first look at a series of other questions you can ask yourself to gauge the seriousness of a behaviour. Each one of these will be followed by recommendations for how you can act upon the answers.

As you already know, behaviour is more or less acceptable according to the context in which it occurs. Thus, running and shouting are perfectly acceptable in a playground context; raising a hand to speak is not a behaviour you would expect in the cafeteria. Context is also related to age and ability, so whereas a nursery age child might want to hold on to your sleeve as you read a story to the class, you would not expect this from a Year 11 pupil; you might expect a child with special needs to communicate in different ways from his or her peers. So a first question to ask when determining whether behaviour is serious enough to warrant intervention is:

- Is this behaviour appropriate for the context in which it is occurring?

Recommendations

School policy and class rules define the behaviours that are acceptable around the school. However, if you are unsure of what constitutes age-appropriate behaviour, especially for an age group you are not used to, try to be observant of the typical behaviour of the whole peer group rather than just the individual whose behaviour is causing you concern. Then ask your supervising teacher or other knowledgeable adult for guidance. If the behaviour is not age- or otherwise context-appropriate, the child needs to be taught – or re-taught – how to behave in that particular situation.

Inappropriate behaviour also tends to draw our attention, so we keep an eye on the pupil who has to be reminded how to behave more than once, and we become more sensitized to repeat instances of misbehaviour from that pupil. We can get the impression that the behaviour is occurring more frequently than is actually the case. Or we may personally find that behaviour particularly annoying, which can also affect our perceptions. So the second question to ask is:

■ How often is this behaviour actually occurring?

Recommendations:
The most obvious way to get an accurate and objective picture of how often a behaviour occurs is to count. Keep a tally of how often you see the behaviour from that child during a 20-minute time period, or during a class. Obviously a child who calls out 20 times in as many minutes is definitely disruptive, and the behaviour has to be dealt with, but you may be surprised to find that the behaviour is not happening quite as frequently as you thought.

Some pupils seem to have a reputation for poor behaviour, and although some of them undoubtedly deserve it, adults and the other children can begin to expect poor behaviour and pick up on every instance of it. In reality other children in the class may be engaging in the same behaviour, but they may be tolerated because they are generally well behaved, or they get their work done despite minor misbehaviours. So the third question to ask is:

■ How does this behaviour compare with that of the other pupils in the group/class?

Recommendations:
To reduce the possibility of bias against pupils known to misbehave, take time to observe other pupils in the group or class, to see if they are behaving in the same way as your 'problem' pupil. If they are, it is a more general behavioural issue and you need to review behavioural expectations with the whole class or group, not just with the individual.

The next question you should ask before attempting to change a pupil's behaviour is a difficult one, because of the complexity of classroom interactions and because it involves your own behaviour. But as a professional you do need to ask:

■ Am I doing something to prompt the behaviour?

Let's look at an example of a very common mistake that adults make:

You ask for a volunteer to take a message to the teacher next door – younger children in particular like to run this sort of errand. You tell your 6-year-old volunteer: 'Go next door to Mrs Wood, please, and tell her that we're not using the hall this afternoon.' He rushes out of the door, anxious to please, only to return a few minutes later to ask: 'What did you want me to tell Mrs Wood?'

The problem here does not lie with the 6 year old. It lies with the multiple instructions: next door, Mrs Wood, not using the hall, this afternoon. So many things for him to forget! He probably went to the right room and said that you had sent him, but that is as far as he got. Like most 6 year olds he could not handle your multiple instructions. Multiple instructions are also difficult for many older children, especially those with attention difficulties. If you give multiple instructions to such children, you set them up to fail in the task you have given them. So if one of your pupils seems to be ignoring your instructions, or doing something he or she has been told not to do, be aware of the part you may have played in triggering that particular behaviour. Ask yourself: Have I caused confusion or difficulties for this pupil because of what I said, or how I said it?

The final question that helps to determine the seriousness of a behaviour is perhaps the most important:

■ Does this behaviour prevent learning taking place?

The line must be drawn at this point. Children do not have to be angels for classrooms to function well and to fulfil their primary purpose. But when behaviour jeopardizes learning – for the pupil who is misbehaving or for other pupils – you must intervene.

Think of a child whose behaviour is causing you concern. Briefly describe that behaviour here. Be as objective as possible in your description of the behaviour.

_____

_____

_____

_____

The Self-evaluation section at the end of the chapter will give you an opportunity to apply these questions to the behaviour of this particular child.

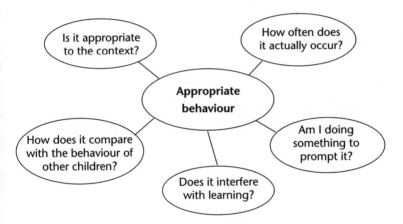

Figure 5.1. Questions that help determine whether behaviour is appropriate

Better behaviour: Being realistic about change

As we have already established, behaviour management is about:

- maintaining behaviour which is already good
- working to prevent and discourage poor behaviour
- improving behaviour which could and should be better.

For most pupils, that means change. Change is an inevitable and integral part of learning, whether children are learning new academic skills or new social skills. The greatest changes will be required of the pupils who have the greatest difficulty following rules and focusing on learning. When you consider trying to change a pupil's behaviour, therefore, you must consider the magnitude of what you are asking that pupil to do. Effective teaching is about moving children along towards greater knowledge and understanding, one small step at a time, building on what they already know and what they can already do. Effective behaviour change must be seen in the same light – you have to build on what a child can already do and what the child already understands, and you can only expect them to change in small increments.

Effective teaching
Building on what a child already knows and what he or she can already do

Effective behaviour change
Building on what a child already knows and what he or she can already do

Change and improvement happen in small increments

Behaviour management plans

In the previous section we talked about the problems that can be caused by adults unwittingly setting children up to fail by setting expectations too high. This is true of changes in behaviour – too often we expect instant, all-round improvement. But we can look at behaviour in two ways:

- frequency (how often it occurs)
- intensity (how extreme it is).

Consider this case:

When David gets frustrated he throws things at other children. He does it several times a day, and he throws whatever comes to hand (stones in the playground, books in the classroom, food in the cafeteria). He rarely manages to hit anyone, but his behaviour obviously needs to change. A behaviour change plan has been set up for David, and he has been told to report to you regularly during the day so that you can check on his progress.

What would you consider to be progress? Jot down three ways in which David's behaviour might improve:

1. _____

2. _____

3. _____

If David had thrown things in class during the morning, but reported that he had thrown no food in the cafeteria at lunchtime, this would certainly qualify as an improvement. If the other children complained that David was flicking paper at them, when he had previously been throwing books, even this would be progress. In the first case, the frequency of the behaviour has reduced, in the second, the intensity. Both constitute progress, and if you were working with a child like David, you should recognize and reward any such progress. They are examples of the 'close approximations' to a desired behaviour that were mentioned in the last chapter – as a child's behaviour moves towards what you want, you reward the improvement, even if it is not yet perfect. Remember the dolphins, and begin by rewarding simple improvements, recognizing and rewarding progress as it occurs.

In terms of helping David to take responsibility for his own behaviour, you can make these things explicit, and let him know that he does not have to be perfectly well behaved in order to be rewarded or praised. You can also work with him to set expectations for change, rather than imposing targets for improvement. He needs to know:

1. that you believe he can behave appropriately
2. that you are willing to recognize his efforts as he works towards that goal
3. that you will consider his opinions and give him some choice in the expectations set for change.

A major component of David's progress is that he is becoming more aware of his own behaviour, which you can also point out to him and praise him for.

Changing pupil behaviour takes determination – on your part, and on the part of the pupil you are working with. You need to acknowledge this when you tackle an unacceptable behaviour, so persist in your intervention, because change also takes time. There will be occasions when a pupil reverts to old behaviours – particularly when under stress (from family circumstances, relationships with peers, finding work difficult – these are all stresses for children and especially for teenagers), but also times when he just spontaneously reacts in old, well-established ways. Consider these minor setbacks as natural glitches. Do not overreact. Remind the pupil of the goals you have jointly set for improvement and recognize positive behaviour as soon as it re-appears.

David's behaviour management plan may be an informal arrangement set up by his class teacher, and for many pupils who have persistent but relatively mild behaviour issues, these informal plans are often enough to improve their behaviour if they are carried out consistently over the course of a few months or a term. However, a pupil whose behaviour is more severe and intrusive will usually have an individualized behaviour plan, often known as an IBP. This may be in conjunction with a statement of special educational needs or individual education plan (IEP), if the behaviour is directly linked to a disability or particular condition. Or it may be stand-alone, if the only issue is behaviour, or the special need is specifically social, emotional and behaviour disorders (SEBD).

It is beyond your jurisdiction as a TA to decide whether a pupil should have a specific behaviour plan. If there is one, your responsibilities for carrying it out should be very clearly defined by your supervising teacher. Formal behaviour plans always have specified goals and objectives for behaviour change, which will guide your expectations. They will also usually specify the methods that you are to use to effect behaviour change. As you work with a child who has a behaviour plan, take note of any difficulties the child is experiencing, as well as his or her successes, so that you can keep your supervising teacher informed, then he or she can make changes if necessary.

Think again about the child you identified whose behaviour is causing you concern. In what ways could that behaviour change for the better? Think in terms of intensity and frequency, as well as the child's attitude to or awareness of his or her behaviour. List some of the possible improvements here:

1. _____

2. _____

3. _____

4. _____

5. _____

Supporting choices and building self-determination

A major role that you play as a TA is to support pupils in the choices they make about how to behave, and in developing self-determination – awareness of their own behaviour and a growing control over it. In this section, we will briefly look at three ways in which you can help children develop self-determination skills:

- teaching children to evaluate their own behaviour in the light of how their peers are behaving
- supporting the development of inductive reasoning
- helping children develop emotional control.

Teaching pupils to evaluate their own behaviour

As we discussed in Chapter 3, pupils learn what is expected of them when teachers establish class rules, and when both teachers and TAs praise and reward appropriate behaviour. You may also have noticed that children take a cue from their peers to see what is expected. This is true of both appropriate and inappropriate behaviour. Pupils will often check to see what others are managing to 'get away with' before misbehaving themselves, but they will also watch for what they are supposed to do. This could be compared with adults, driving along an unfamiliar road, who see signs for speed cameras. They gauge whether they should slow down by the extent to which other drivers modify their speed. If everyone slows down to the speed limit, this is a pretty sure indicator that fines or penalties are regularly issued against drivers found speeding there. If no one seems to slow down it is reasonable to assume that the cameras operate only infrequently and the risk of penalties for speeding is low.

If you have a child who is not doing as he or she should, you can use the natural tendency to follow the lead of peers, to prompt that child to evaluate his or her own behaviour. In the previous chapter, one of the supportive discipline measures listed was to praise good behaviour in another pupil, but for pupils who cannot seem to pick up on such a subtle hint, you can take a more direct approach.

Take for example a classroom where all the pupils are sitting at their desks, except John, who is wandering around. You might simply say:

> 'John, can you see what the others are doing? They're sitting down and working. What should you be doing?'
>
> [John answers]
>
> 'Yes, sitting at your desk and working. So sit down and get on with your work, please.'

What you are effectively doing is modelling the type of conversation you would like John to have with himself, which would lead to his modifying his own behaviour. In the self-evaluation section at the end of Chapter 4 you had an opportunity to craft some positive responses to common inappropriate behaviours, re-phrasing the responses as positive, corrective teaching statements rather than demands or rebukes. This is essentially the same type of technique.

Supporting the development of inductive reasoning

Inductive reasoning is the process of realizing that what you have done has affected someone else. The effect can be positive or negative. This concept is usually taught at home in a child's early years, as when a parent points out to the child, 'See what you've done? You took your brother's toy and now he's crying.' This translation or interpretation of what has happened helps the child to see the result of his or her action:

> I took his toy, and that's why he's crying.

However it is also important to link in the emotion that the other child is feeling:

> You took his toy – that made him sad – he's crying because he's sad – and that means you caused the sadness by taking his toy.

Teaching inductive reasoning is a beginning step towards helping children develop empathy, because they learn to interpret how the other person feels. It also teaches them responsibility for their actions, because they learn to see that they caused the hurt or distress. Many adolescents have not developed this important ability to put themselves in someone else's place and take responsibility for the negative consequences that they have caused. Although they will have been taught this concept in their early years in school, they may need to be reminded of it, and helped to see that they can avoid getting themselves and other pupils into trouble by anticipating the possible consequences of their own actions, and choosing not to behave in that way. And remember that you can help children develop inductive reasoning by pointing out the positive instances as well as the negative: making the same type of explicit connections when they behave in a way that is helpful or supportive to another child.

Helping pupils develop emotional control

Healthy emotional development is critical to happiness and a feeling of success. Many children come to school with emotional baggage which neither teachers nor TAs can remove or change. But you can help to establish school as a positive environment where children feel secure enough to recognize – and then learn to control – their emotions.

First, you can be honest about your own feelings. You can be openly enthusiastic about the good things that happen, expressing how you feel in specific terms:

> 'You worked really hard on those maths problems – I'm proud of you.'

'You've handed your homework in every day so far this week – I'm looking forward to awarding you free time when you hand it in again tomorrow.'

When less positive things happen, you can also honestly express what you feel.

'I'm disappointed to hear you've been fighting again.'
'I'm sorry you've got to stay in at break time.'

Even if you are expressing negative emotions, this is helpful because children want to know that they matter and that you care about them, even if they have disappointed you. And if you can tell them why you are disappointed or frustrated –

. . . because I know you can do better, or
. . . because I know you want to be able to go on the school trip.

This adds a positive note that shows the emotions are founded on your concern for them.

Second, when feelings run high you can talk about it with your pupils. Here is a common example:

A disagreement arises between two pupils, and you intervene. You take them aside and ask them to take turns telling you about the disagreement. You let each child give his or her own version of the story without interruption, then you tell them what the consequences will be.

You can also help each child to name the emotions they are experiencing, and acknowledge their right to feeling that way.

'He took your book without asking and it was torn when he gave it back? No wonder you're angry.'

You then need to explain that although they have the right to the emotion, they must carefully choose how they react to it because in choosing their reactions they choose the consequences. You can then talk them through potential alternative solutions for dealing with the situation.

The purpose for this type of teaching interaction is to lead pupils through a problem-solving process so that as they mature, they will be able to identify their emotions and find their own solutions for conflicts and challenges. Of course, not all events which cause emotions can be resolved so easily, and you should not put yourself in a position of offering counselling to a child about a situation that really should be dealt with by a mental health professional. Particularly if a child who is upset tells you about events that relate to abuse or other child protection, you must refer it to your supervising teacher as soon as possible. If you are unsure of your responsibilities relating to child protection, or want more information about it, you can search the government's Teachernet website (www.teachernet.gov.uk) using the term 'child protection'.

Emotional self-regulation is an important skill for young people. It is a learned skill and it requires voluntary management of emotions. As you model your own emotional self-regulatory skills, your pupils will be more likely to learn emotional self-regulation themselves. You do this every time you deal with inappropriate behaviour in a calm and reasonable manner. The child knows that his or her behaviour may have been irritating or frustrating to you, but every time you refuse to get angry or impatient you model emotional self-regulation. You can tell a child, 'It's very frustrating for me to see you getting into trouble so often', so that they understand that you are dealing with an emotion but are refusing to let it dictate negative behaviour on your part.

It may be helpful to understand some of the phases that pupils naturally go through as they develop these skills. The table describes the different stages.

Pupils' behaviour strategies	Phase
Stage 1 Pupils do not have effective strategies to help them monitor their work or behaviour. Behaviour is spontaneous and unreasoned.	Nursery
Stage 2 Pupils begin to develop awareness and strategies, but are inconsistent in the implementation of strategies to control their actions.	Early years
Stage 3 Pupils begin to use strategies well, but their behaviour can revert to that of an earlier stage as increasing demands are made on them.	Primary
Stage 4 Pupils know strategies and can use them effectively. Those who are good at self-regulation are more successful academically.	Secondary

Table 5.1. Developing behaviour strategies

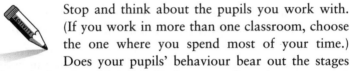

Stop and think about the pupils you work with. (If you work in more than one classroom, choose the one where you spend most of your time.) Does your pupils' behaviour bear out the stages described in the table? Are all of your pupils at the same stage? Write some thoughts here:

_____

_____

_____

_____

Best behaviour: Keeping pupils motivated

In Chapter 1 we referred to Maslow's Hierarchy, or the pyramid of needs that Abraham Maslow suggested that we all have. These progress from the most basic need for physical comfort and safety, to the more complex and sophisticated needs for love and a sense of belonging, self-esteem and self-actualization – or the sense of having the power to act as an independent individual, and being able to influence what goes on around us. This pyramid of needs represents a growing independence. Whereas babies and young children rely on others to meet their basic needs, as we grow and mature we take more responsibility for meeting our own needs and become more able to guide our own lives. According to their age and level of maturity, the children you work with will be at different stages in relation to the levels or items on the hierarchy, but what is motivating for them is to be given opportunities to move up, as it were, and take on new challenges and increasing independence, in a supportive environment.

Inappropriate behaviour often stems from:

- boredom (when classroom life offers too few challenges)
- frustration (when tasks are perceived as too difficult, or when children feel powerless to achieve)
- fear (particularly the fear of failing and looking foolish).

Children behave appropriately when they feel they can cope with their work and the social demands made on them, and when they have a clear picture of what those demands are.

Maslow's Hierarchy of Needs

Self-actualization
Esteem
Love and belonging
Safety
Physiological needs

Through Chapters 2, 3 and 4 we have discussed many of the ways in which you can challenge your pupils to change and mature, while giving them the necessary support:

- Setting reasonable expectations for behaviour and clearly stating the benefits when they meet the expectations, as well as the more negative consequences of not meeting expectations.
- Using supportive discipline techniques to remind and guide pupils' actions.
- Offering and providing attractive rewards for appropriate behaviour.
- Imposing pre-agreed sanctions when necessary.
- Teaching children that they can choose how to behave and therefore choose the consequences.
- Providing stimulating work set at the right level for pupil abilities and interests.

Through the preceding sections of this chapter we have added to the supportive techniques you can use to motivate your pupils. A clear, reasonable and consistent approach to all of these aspects of behaviour management helps children to be motivated to behave appropriately. It also provides your pupils with a model of competence and power, which they will want to emulate, because self-esteem is based on knowing what you want and knowing how to achieve it. As a TA you know what you and your supervising teacher want in terms of behaviour from your pupils, and you know the strategies and techniques you can use to make that happen.

One of the very practical ways in which you can motivate your pupils is to offer them choices. When adults make the majority of decisions for children, it robs the children of the opportunity for making choices and learning from the results. It often seems easier and less complicated in the short term to impose our preferences on children, but in the long term it is unhelpful to them.

Think of some examples of choices you give your pupils. If you cannot think of many, try and think of additional ways in which you could offer them choice.

Write your thoughts here:

_____

_____

_____

_____

As a TA you obviously cannot give pupils the choice of whether they come to class, when they have break or – particularly in secondary school – what subjects they study. But within the set boundaries of timetables, curriculum content and your assigned duties with the children, there are many opportunities for choice. Consider these possibilities:

- If two things must be completed within a certain time period, the child may be able to choose which to do first. Even the choice between whether to write the story or draw the picture first is a possibility. We have children illustrate their work as a type of reward and added extra, but the creative act of drawing is a good tool for prompting ideas for writing, so it can work in reverse of what is typical. Let them know that they must work on both, and give clear time limits so that they know they cannot linger over the picture at the expense of the writing.

- Children can often be given a choice of which reward they would like for completing their work or behaving in a particular way. This cannot of course be a totally open choice, but you can usually give them choice from a small menu of possibilities – free time or house points, playing in the sand-pit or the water.

- To allow for personal preferences, children can often be given the choice of whether to work alone or in collaboration with another pupil. This is obviously not true of all activities or tasks, but can work well for science or craft projects, shared reading or project work. In addition to enjoying the freedom of choice, children get an opportunity to practise collaborative skills.

These sorts of small opportunities to choose can give children a sense of power and influence in the classroom. Most children recognize the authority that rightly belongs to adults, and are willing to submit to prescribed routines and ways of working or behaving. But it is worthwhile including them in decision making whenever it is feasible, both because it is motivating for them, and because it helps them to develop their own decision-making skills.

Chapter summary

This chapter has been about change, but it has focused on three areas:

1. When you should be trying to change behaviour – that is, when is it sufficiently serious to warrant intervention?
2. How much change to expect, and how quickly to expect it to happen.
3. How to motivate and support pupils in making changes.

This included suggestions of how to increase levels of self-determination for your pupils – by modelling self-evaluation for them, helping them to use inductive reasoning and develop emotional control. In the case of pupils whose behaviour is acceptable and appropriate, you may feel that no change is needed. But all pupils should be moving forward in their development – socially and academically – so even if the child is already well behaved, change is still needed in terms of growing emotional maturity and self-determination. And you can support that growth and development as you help to provide a positive learning environment where pupils feel valued, and have opportunities to make choices about their work.

Self-evaluation

Look back at the behaviour of concern that you briefly described earlier in the chapter. Describe the behaviour again, but this time include the emotional impact that it has on you (frustration, anger, etc.) and the reasons for those emotions. For example, 'I get really frustrated when Jordan does . . . because . . .'

_____

_____

_____

_____

Now in each of the following statements, circle the option which applies to the behaviour.

This behaviour is / is not appropriate to the context in which it is occurring.

This behaviour occurs [say how often]

This behaviour is /is not similar to the behaviour of the child's peers.

This behaviour is / is not prompted by something I am doing.

This behaviour is / is not interfering with learning.

If your teacher asked you to summarize the seriousness of the behaviour in 40 words or fewer, what would you say, given the answers to the questions above?

_____

_____

_____

_____

_____

In the light of this assessment, and based on the information that you have gained from this book and other sources, think of some options for the action you could take to reduce or eliminate the behaviour. Make a note of your options here. (If you find that you are at a complete loss to know what to do, talk to your supervising teacher – this may well be a behaviour that you cannot possibly handle alone.)

1. _____

_____

2. _____

_____

3. _____

_____

Now think of the emotional impacts of the behaviour, and make a note of what you could say or do to model emotional self-regulation, while dealing with the behaviour.

_____

_____

_____

_____

Conclusion

And so we are almost at the end of this book on managing children's behaviour. Let's take a look at the topics we have covered so far.

To begin with, we considered why behaviour management would be a necessary topic for you as a TA. The primary reason for this is that as an adult who works with children you are constantly faced with different behaviours from your pupils, and you must respond to them. How you respond has a direct influence on whether they then behave appropriately or not. When you first began your job as a TA you may have had very definite ideas on how children should behave, and how you would react to their behaviour, or you may be more of a 'see how it goes' type of person who lets things happen before you decide what should be done. Whichever is the case, you have been managing behaviour – systematically or spontaneously, well or poorly – from the first day that you began your work as a TA.

Early on in the book we also considered the fact that behaviour management is not just a question of dealing with inappropriate behaviour. This book has been about behaviour management, or learning behaviour, as the Steer Report termed it – that is, having a system in place that encourages and maintains positive behaviour, with a Plan B for when behaviours are poor or challenging. As a TA you work under the direction of a qualified and designated supervisor, but you know that you cannot leave behaviour management to your supervisor – you must have your own authority with your pupils and that comes from being well prepared and confident about directing their behaviour and ensuring that there are appropriate consequences.

Take a moment to think about your role in managing children's behaviour, in light of what you have learned. Has your perspective on children's behaviour changed? Do you see your role in a different light?

_____

_____

_____

_____

_____

_____

In Chapter 1 we looked at some different theoretical or philosophical perspectives of behaviour and its causes, and how these apply to a classroom situation. In particular, we looked at:

- The psychodynamic approach, with its origins in psychoanalysis, psychiatry and medicine. This approach has its limitations for school settings because of the emphasis on therapy and the need to analyse the deeper motivations and urges that prompt us to behave in particular ways.

- The behavioural approach, which sees behaviour as a response to stimuli in the environment. This forms the basis of the ABCs that we looked at in Chapter 2, and takes the very practical approach that if we change antecedents and consequences, we can generally change behaviour.

■ The cognitive behavioural approach, which sees behaviour as a set of social skills which pupils can learn in the same way that they learn academic skills.

The question 'What is acceptable behaviour?' highlighted the fact that context plays a major part in determining whether actions are appropriate or not. This includes a child's age, abilities and culture. Nevertheless, certain behaviours are never acceptable in school. And whatever a child's needs, ability level or culture, it is not only possible but also essential to teach them to behave appropriately in the classroom and around the school.

Take a moment to think back over these issues of culture and ability, and how they relate to the children you work with. How have you changed your expectations and your approach to the behaviour of your pupils in light of what you have learned?

In Chapter 2 we learned our ABCs – the Antecedents or triggers for Behaviour, and the Consequences, good and bad, which might follow. This was where we looked at how you can use antecedents and consequences to shape children's actions, as you remove triggers to negative behaviour and offer real incentives for positive behaviour. We also made the point that behaviour is a matter of choice, and that we need to teach children this principle, so that they understand that they can choose their own consequences as they carefully choose how to act.

What changes will you make (or have you already made) as a result of learning your ABCs?

In Chapter 3 we looked at how we set expectations for behaviour:

1. through a whole-school policy
2. by establishing routines and setting rules for the classroom.

These are likely to be beyond your control as a TA. But one of the most important techniques at your disposal to help maintain positive behaviour is using effective teaching methods:

■ setting work at a level and pace that suit the children you work with
■ presenting information in interesting and varied ways
■ organizing physical space to minimize distractions and increase efficiency.

The other important technique that helps maintain a positive learning environment is developing positive relationships with your pupils. Remember the analogy of a bank account: you make deposits through the small and simple things you do to show your pupils that you are interested in them, and are willing to invest your time and efforts in their success. To this end we looked at how the ABCs apply to your behaviour as an adult –

how you can learn to recognize what triggers your own behaviour, so that you can take the necessary steps to ensure that consequences are as positive as possible for you and your pupils.

Use the graphic to remind yourself of the ways in which building strong relationships promotes a positive learning environment and appropriate behaviour.

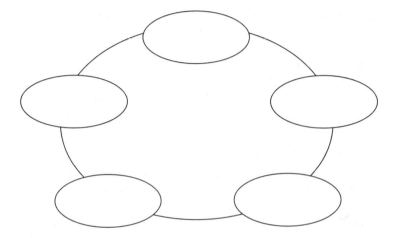

Figure C.1. Ways in which strong relationships promote positive behaviour

In Chapter 4 we looked at rewards and sanctions. First you took some time to think about how you can support your teacher's incentive plan – the types of rewards that are available for your pupils, and the extent to which you have authority to offer rewards. But because the notion of a reward is so subjective, we spent some time looking at the types of rewards your pupils respond well to, and also considering whether it is possible to give too many rewards. Remember the principles we learned from the dolphin trainer:

1. Start simply
2. Recognize and support progress
3. Keep doling out the fish.

Most of what we discussed to this point in the book related to preventive or supportive discipline – the measures you take to establish, encourage and maintain positive behaviour. The remainder of the chapter looked at corrective discipline measures and some of the principles involved in imposing sanctions when that becomes necessary. You also took some time to think about bullying and what your responsibilities and authority are for when you see instances of this particularly unacceptable behaviour.

 Many of the principles we discussed in this chapter may already be part of your repertoire, so take a moment to fill in the columns with actions you already take that constitute preventive, supportive and corrective discipline. Add any that you intend to adopt as a result of your reading and learning.

Preventive discipline measures	Supportive discipline measures	Corrective discipline measures

Table C.1. Preventive, supportive and corrective discipline measures I can use

In Chapter 5 we looked at how you can help children take responsibility for their own behaviour, or develop self-determination. First we looked at a series of questions you can ask when confronted with a particular behaviour, to decide how serious it really is. These related to

■ context
■ frequency
■ similarity to the behaviour of peers
■ whether you as an adult were causing some of the difficulties
■ most importantly, the extent to which the behaviour impedes learning.

In the next section of the chapter you looked at the realities of change – that although it is a constant necessity in the process of learning, we must acknowledge the enormous challenge that it presents for some pupils, and adjust our expectations accordingly.

When pupil behaviour is severe or persistent enough, it may warrant a behaviour management plan. Whether this is an informal arrangement set up by the teacher or a more formal IBP, if you are working with a pupil who has a behaviour plan, your support will be critical. As you recognize progress of any kind – including the pupil's growing awareness of his or her own behaviour – you will be helping to effect behaviour change. This led us on to a brief discussion of self-determination – ways in which you can help pupils become more aware of and more responsible for their own behaviour. This is really one of the major purposes of teaching children appropriate behaviour – so that they can take over from us, as it were, and take charge of how they choose to behave. The first step in this process is to make them more aware of their behaviour, and of the fact that they can choose how to react to situations and people rather than feeling forced to behave in particular ways.

List here one of the ways in which you could help to develop self-determination in a pupil whose behaviour is a cause for concern. What does that pupil most need? What would be most helpful for him or her, in changing an inappropriate behaviour?

_____

_____

_____

_____

_____

_____

Some general principles

This book has been about managing behaviour – good and bad, yours and that of your pupils. Here are some basic principles which you can keep in mind as you undertake this important role:

1. Children's behaviour is influenced by many different factors, and you have control over only a few of those factors. You cannot change or remove from their lives all of the negative influences they may be subject to. What you can change and use to good advantage is the environment in which you and the children spend your time. So learn to manage behaviour in the areas over which you have control, using the resources that are available to you.

2. Even though children may have many negative influences in their lives, this does not excuse them from behaving appropriately in school. Nor does it excuse you from trying to modify their inappropriate behaviour by teaching them how to behave more appropriately. You can be

encouraged by the fact that most children and teenagers survive against all the odds and grow up to be successful and confident adults. You can assist that process.

3. A very basic principle of effective behaviour management is consistency – between you and your teacher or other adults who work in the classroom, and consistency when you manage behaviour as an individual on a daily basis. There are times when discipline can be relaxed, but in general you must maintain a steady response to behaviours. Those that are considered totally unacceptable should never be ignored or tolerated; acceptable behaviour should consistently receive a positive response. And lastly, there must be consistency between assertions and behaviour – you must practise what you preach. If you tell pupils to raise their hand before answering a question, but you respond to the first child who blurts out an answer, you have not followed your own rule and have told your pupils in effect that the rule is unimportant.

4. Keep it simple. Picture this: You are driving along in the car, and you feel too hot. What do you do? You switch off the heater and open the window. Before long, of course, you are feeling decidedly chilly. So you close the window and turn the heater back on. In truth, you could either have switched off the heater, or opened the window. Doing both has produced a negative effect. Apply this to managing behaviour. One of your pupils has a persistent, mildly disruptive behaviour that needs to be corrected. When you decide what to do about it, there is no need to make complicated plans and use your whole repertoire of behaviour management skills. Keep it simple (the American version is *KISS* – Keep It Simple, Stupid). Use the minimal intervention possible. It may well be enough.

5. The supportive discipline measures that we looked at in Chapter 4 consist firstly of subtle hints or cues for behaviour. Some children do not pick up these cues and have to have the principle or concept spelled out for them – which

is what you do when you teach inductive reasoning or teach a child to self-evaluate. Be alert to the child who misses the subtle hint and support him by being explicit about what you want him to do, and about the cues that he is missing. Your gentle but clear reminders will eventually register and resound in his mind when he is faced by choices in how to behave.

General principles:

1. You do not have control over all of the influences on a child's behaviour; work on those that you can control.
2. Assume that all children can learn to behave; assume the responsibility for teaching them.
3. Be consistent – with your teacher's approach, in responding to pupils and in practising what you preach.
4. Keep it simple – use single, low-intensity interventions first.
5. Be explicit if children cannot pick up on available cues.

Children want to be accepted – they want to belong. They are willing to belong to a learning community, if that learning community is willing to accept them, and support them, and acknowledge their efforts. They want to succeed. Your contribution to the behaviour management of the learning community where you work can be substantial, and can help ensure their success.

Appendix

In this appendix you will find information on further resources for behaviour management, useful websites and recommendations for further reading.

Resources

A wide variety of resources is available relating to behaviour management, and you can access these in a variety of ways. They include books, professional journals and magazines, and professional organizations.

Books

Thousands of books have been written about behaviour management. Your teacher or professional supervisor may have some that you could dip into; or your local library, especially in the section on parenting and child development. There is also a growing number of books such as this one written specifically for TAs, so keep an eye out for new titles. Here is a list of relevant publishers:

Continuum

www.continuumbooks.com
This book is part of Continuum's Teaching Assistant series. You can click on *View series titles* on the website home page and scroll down to this series. Other series that relate to education include: *Continuum One Hundreds*, *Special Educational Needs*, and *Supporting Children* (this one is especially

for TAs). In the general education catalogue you will also find *101 Essential Lists for Teaching Assistants*.

Paul Chapman Publishing
www.paulchapmanpublishing.co.uk
This publisher lists a large number of books relating to behaviour management, and also lists a number of books that would be useful for TAs – although they are not necessarily written specifically with TAs in mind. Two books you might be interested in are *Positive Approaches to Disruption in School* and *Resolving Behaviour Problems in your School: A Practical Guide for Teachers and Support Staff*.

Sage Publications
www.sagepub.co.uk
Sage offers several books on behaviour management, although none of them is written specifically for TAs. A search on the Sage website using the term 'teaching assistant' will bring up a good list of books, including two which are specifically for TAs: *A Toolkit for the Effective Teaching Assistant* and *Supporting Children's Learning*.

Learning Matters
www.learningmatters.co.uk
Learning Matters has two series of particular interest to TAs: the Teaching Assistants' Handbooks, which includes *Supporting Learning in Primary Schools*, and the Higher Level Teaching Assistants series.

A search on the www.amazon.co.uk website using the term teaching assistant will also bring up a range of books written for TAs from a variety of publishers.

Professional journals and magazines
Again, your supervisor may subscribe to a professional publication that could have relevant items, or your school may have

a subscription, so check the staffroom shelf, or ask your supervising teacher if he or she knows of anything that is available around the school. There is now a magazine specifically for TAs called *Learning Support*, which regularly includes articles on behaviour management. You can subscribe to the magazine as an individual or a school can take out an institutional subscription. Information can be found on the website: www.learningsupport.co.uk

Professional organizations

Many of the professional teaching organizations and unions now offer membership to TAs. Even without membership you can usually access basic information on their websites and they often include information on government reports or legislation and policy. Here is a selection of teacher associations and their websites:

- Association of Teachers and Lecturers (ATL), www.atl.org.uk
- National Association of Schoolmasters Union of Women Teachers (NASUWT), www.nasuwt.org.uk
- National Association for Special Educational Needs (NASEN), www.nasen.org.uk
- National Union of Teachers (NUT), www.teachers.org.uk
- Professional Association of Teachers (PAT), www.pat.org.uk

  PAT includes PANN, the Professional Association of Nursery Nurses, and PAtT (Professionals Allied to Teaching – i.e. support staff).

Useful websites

The following websites offer useful information on behaviour management.

www.behaviouruk.com

This is a website offering many practical behaviour management resources and a chat room where you can join discussions about behavioural issues. Among the resources are:

1. *Playing Up Again*, a pack of ten short play scripts that can be used in assembly or class to teach appropriate behaviour.
2. *School Detention Papers: Re-Thinking My Behaviour* – almost 500 photocopiable pages that can be used with pupils in detention, or as behaviour support for individuals. They are designed to get pupils to think about their inappropriate behaviour, why they behaved as they did, and what the consequences were. Pages cover specific misdemeanours, such as: Swearing/Inappropriate Language, Teasing & Bullying, The Importance of Rules, Racial Unkindness, I Have Not Been Doing My Homework.

These resources are fairly expensive as they are intended for schools to purchase, but it is important for you to be aware of what is available, and you can download a sample of each one from the website.

www.behaviour4learning.ac.uk

This is a site supported by the TDA (Teaching and Development Agency for Schools). It offers a large number of resources and practical suggestions for managing behaviour. This website also provides links to examples of whole-school behaviour policies.

www.dfes.gov.uk
This is the Department for Education and Skills (DfES) website, where you can access information on the 1989 Elton Report, as well as many other government documents.

www.dfes.gov.uk/behaviourandattendance/about/learning_ behaviour.cfm
You can access the full text of the Steer Report (*Learning Behaviour: The Report of the Practitioners' Group on School Behaviour and Discipline*) on these pages of the DfES website.

www.ofsted.gov.uk
This is the website for the Office for Standards in Education, or Ofsted, the government body responsible for inspecting schools. You can access the 2005 report *Managing Challenging Behaviour* by following these links from the home page: Publications and Research > Browse all by Title > then Click on the letter 'M'.

www.tda.gov.uk
This is the website for the Training and Development Agency for Schools. Two items of interest on this site are:

1. The Induction training for TAs in England. The full training materials can be downloaded by following the links: Support staff > Learning support staff > Qualifications and training > Induction and introductory training > Training material downloads. There are separate materials for primary and secondary schools, but both have a section entitled *Promoting Positive Behaviour.*
2. The 2000 government document: *Working with Teaching Assistants: A Good Practice Guide.* Written for heads and teachers, but plenty of good information for TAs as well.

Further reading

Susan Bentham has written several books for TAs, among them *A Teaching Assistant's Guide to Managing Behaviour in the Classroom*. Publisher: Routledge Falmer.

Glenys Fox has written several books for TAs, in particular *Supporting Children with Behaviour Difficulties: A Guide for Assistants in Schools*. The publisher was David Fulton, but information about the book can more easily be accessed through www.amazon.co.uk rather than directly through the current publisher, Routledge.

Karen Pryor is a behavioural psychologist who spent many years training animals, including dolphins. Her book *On Behavior* is a more general book about behaviour, but it makes for fascinating light reading. You might start with the chapters 'The Rhino likes Violets' and 'A Gathering of Birds' before moving on to the more formal research chapters. Publisher: Sunshine Books.

Harry K. Wong is an American author with a very practical and detailed approach to behaviour management. He and his wife Rosemary T. Wong have written *The First Days of School: How to Be an Effective Teacher*. Although the book is written primarily for an American audience, the principles are universally useful, and the book is written in a very practical and user-friendly style. Publisher: Harry K. Wong Publications.

Ted Wragg (Edward C. Wragg) was a long-time education columnist in the *Guardian* and the *Times Education Supplement* (TES), and also wrote many books relating to education. *Class Management in the Primary School* and *Class Management in the Secondary School* are both very practical guides to managing behaviour and are available from Routledge, www.routledge.com.